Fast Forward Your Career

Fast Forward Your Career

A Personal Playbook to Boost Leadership

Simonetta Lureti and Lucio Furlani

BEP

BUSINESS EXPERT PRESS

Leader in applied, concise business books

Fast Forward Your Career: A Personal Playbook to Boost Leadership

Copyright © Business Expert Press, LLC, 2022.

Illustrations and cover design by Sebastiano Boni

Interior design by Exeter Premedia Services Private Ltd., Chennai, India

First published in 2021 by
Business Expert Press, LLC
222 East 46th Street, New York, NY 10017
www.businessexpertpress.com

ISBN-13: 978-1-63742-103-1 (paperback)
ISBN-13: 978-1-63742-104-8 (e-book)

Business Expert Press Business Career Development Collection

Collection ISSN: 2642-2123 (print)
Collection ISSN: 2642-2131 (electronic)

First edition: 2021

10 9 8 7 6 5 4 3 2 1

To my grandpa,
Simonetta

To my wife, Francesca
The perfect companion,
Lucio

Description

Fast Forward Your Career is for managers, corporate staff, and MBA students who want to position themselves for their next career opportunity and learn the necessary skills to be successful in the digital age.

Human is at the core, the business has adapted, and organizations are more open, flat, and fluid. The concept of leadership evolves. Business acumen and execution continue to be pivotal. But alone, they are not enough to achieve success. The ability to listen, create trust, and work with purpose become enablers of one-on-one engagement, high performance, self-realization.

A new mindset is needed to face the unknown. New skills such as creativity, antifragility, emotional intelligence, and critical thinking have to be practiced to boost true leadership, inspire and motivate people, and grab opportunities in these uncertain times. Communication and collaboration at all levels, across and outside the organization, are key for your career.

In this book, the authors provide a useful, practical, and intuitive guide to important topics, often mentioned, not always known, but fundamental to develop your leadership skills and guide your career in the digital age. They have condensed their experience as executives, coaches, consultants to challenge you with insights and further application. The book combines practical concepts with storytelling to let you observe skills in practice. Interviews with successful leaders bring further proof and additional perspectives on effective leadership. Finally, an introduction to the Science of Happiness shares recent findings that cannot be ignored by leaders and organizations in the postpandemic scenario.

Keywords

career development; leader; leadership; leadership style; skill; coach; trust; purpose; true leadership; team management; emotional intelligence; effective leadership; uncertainty; mindset; science of happiness

Contents

Introduction

We are in the digital age: Technology pervades our lives, data drive product and service design, and customer experience becomes a strategic objective. Innovation is pivotal to differentiate and win in the "ocean" of competition.

In this scenario, boundaries widen, relationships go beyond the company perimeter, and the collaboration with customers, suppliers, and, in general, with the market becomes key to success. COVID-19 has made us more and more digital: virtual, distant, and isolated in the new normal.

The concept of leadership must evolve. Business acumen and execution continue to be pivotal. But alone, they are not enough to achieve success. The ability to listen, create trust, and work with purpose become enablers of one-on-one engagement, high performance, and self-realization.

A new mindset is needed to face the unknown. New skills such as creativity, antifragility, emotional intelligence, and critical thinking have to be practiced to boost true leadership, inspire and motivate people, and grab opportunities in these uncertain times.

The working environment turns out to be open, fluid, and agile in response to market needs—communication and collaboration at all levels, across and outside the organization, are key for your career.

The concept of teams also changes. People come together and disband based on projects, extending beyond traditional hierarchical boundaries. Executives become facilitators, directors who choose the best actors for their projects, creating virtual teams with functional skills for their goals. They are also connectors introducing their coworkers to colleagues who need specific skills.

The hierarchical relationship between executives and collaborators flattens out: Mutual feedback allows for effective relationships and best-in-class business outcomes; trust and engagement enable remote relationships.

In this dynamic environment, it becomes increasingly important to find purpose in daily activities and ensure that each employee works in alignment with their deepest needs. "Doing without being" does not allow for sustainable success overtime.

This book was born in this context, with the belief that now, more than ever, executives must know a broad, interdisciplinary set of skills to be successful in this fluid and highly dynamic digital environment. They must be coaches, knowing how to listen, communicate, and empower collaborators, earning their trust, and relating with empathy. They must be mentors, sharing experiences and encouraging a new mindset focused on growth and continuous learning. Finally, they must be consultants, strategizing and executing initiatives, knowing contemporary approaches, using tools, and reading data effectively.

Each chapter is dedicated to one skill and presents:

- The story to observe the skill in action
- The theory to provide a theoretical deep dive about the skill

The story told in this book is the result of fiction, albeit influenced by the experience of the authors. Facts, people, and places that emerge from the experience have inspired the narrative. However, any relation with real characters and situations is purely coincidental. Similarly, the deep dives share the authors' personal view if not specified alternatively.

The book ends with 2 appendixes:

- few interviews with successful executives who bring their authentic testimony of leadership
- an introduction to the Science of Happiness. Due to the pandemic, leaders and organizations should not ignore its clear benefits.

By writing this book, the authors want to provide managers, corporate staff, and MBA students a useful, practical, and intuitive guide to fundamental topics, often mentioned, not always known, but key for positioning the next career opportunity and learning the necessary skills to be successful in the digital age. We have condensed our experience as executives, coaches, and consultants in the IT world to challenge you with insights and further application.

To you, enjoy the reading!

Simonetta and Lucio

Review Quotes

"In Fast Forward Your Career, Simonetta and Lucio present an engaging Business Management narrative (book) on leadership—both the latest theories and practical implementations. They offer a framework for success told through real life examples, (and great characters) showing what managers and executives must do to become emotionally intelligent and successful leaders. Thoroughly enjoyable and a go to for me in future assignments."—**Neta Tully**

"Effective, easy, and relevant. This book is a practical guide to develop key, interdisciplinary skills for the Leaders of tomorrow. Read, apply, and progress in your career."—**Lorenzo Savioli**

"Engaging case story, interspersed with theoretical drill-downs on necessary soft and hard skills to succeed in today's business world. Incisive and full of information. Great reading for master students and middle managers who aspire to take more senior roles."—**Enrique Salmona**

Acknowledgments

This book was born in front of a pizza, a Wednesday of 1 year ago.

We have known each other for almost 20 years and have worked together for 2, being united by mutual respect and esteem.

This book is the result of our professional experience, the people we met, the training we did. When we thought about the topic, our experiences came together, we put aspiring leaders at the center, and we asked ourselves what they needed to develop their skills, step forward in their career, and develop their leadership. The answer guided us in writing this book.

This book would not have existed without the people we met along our path.

We want to thank the friends and colleagues who granted us the interviews: Letizia Mariani, Marco Airoldi, and Andrea Cardillo. Your experience has enriched the book with different and personal perspectives.

We also thank those who dedicated their time to us, reading our draft and sharing important feedback to make it better: Neta Tully, Luca Sighinolfi, Enrique Salmona, Lorenzo Savioli.

Special thanks also go to Sebastiano, our designer, who managed to give shape to our words!

A huge thank you also goes to our publisher, Business Express Press (BEP), for believing in us and recognizing the value of our project: Scott Isenberg and Vilma Barr for their valuable advice; Charlene Kronstedt, our super helpful Director of Production; and Melissa Yeager, Editorial and Marketing Operations officer. For us, "young" Italian authors, it is an honor to be able to publish with you. Your preparation, availability, kindness have made our collaboration much easier.

Finally, a special thanks goes to our families for supporting and enduring us in the creation of this book.

Simonetta and Lucio

CHAPTER 1

The Assignment

Boston, Sunday, 11:00 a.m.

It is late March, the weather is mild, and Thomas and Luke went out for a stroll. Katherine is finally alone at home: free to slow down, relax, and think about herself.

As it always happens when you want to "disconnect," your mind brings you back to work. And so it happened to Katherine who went back to the meeting planned for the next morning. Her boss had scheduled a meeting with the COO (chief operating officer), without providing any detail. Why? What do they want to tell her?

Katherine has been a manager for a while. She is satisfied with her job and her reputation. People say she is transparent, honest, and direct. But that is not enough—she wants more, she is ambitious. She believes that her career has reached a critical point: She is at the turning point. She knows she has all the credentials to aspire to a promotion. That would mean status, money, and a broader ability to influence business decisions.

She is already 37 and she cannot remember anyone who has been promoted to director over 40.

She oversees the Marketing Analytics team and she really likes it. She has built positive relationships with everyone in the team and, above all, she has great respect for her manager Alessandra, the company's chief marketing officer. She would like to grow and be promoted, but Alessandra is unknowingly a "roadblock." She is 45 years old, in the role for 6 years, after a multiyear experience as the leader for international markets. Alessandra is too young and too good to aspire to take her place.

However, Katherine doesn't want to give up: She has a wonderful curriculum, a lot of experience, and a good network. To make the leap, she needs the right combination of will and luck.

Strongly rooted in Massachusetts, her company—Apold International—has an international scope, a quite respectable market presence, and several hundred employees. Thirty years of activity, a leadership team between 50 and 60 years old, with a uniform, conservative management style. True, Apold is not particularly innovative, but overall it is a solid firm, with an enjoyable working environment and where those who are good can stand out.

Katherine's mind turns back again to tomorrow's meeting. It was set up only last Thursday and this surprised her. Worried a bit. Not sure what to expect. She knows the COO mostly by reputation as she has only met him a couple of times: He seems an old-fashioned executive with somewhat rigid ideas.

When she asked her boss for more information, Alessandra was rather evasive: "Katherine, don't worry. It's simply a meeting: We want to share some ideas with you."

But what ideas will they be? The company is solid, but it is losing market share. It may be time for a strategic change or more drastic decisions. Katherine cannot stop thinking about it. What will the COO want from her?

***

Monday, 7:30 a.m.

Katherine leaves her apartment and takes Luke to school before heading to the office.

She loves to do it every morning, greeting and wishing him a wonderful day of learning new stuff, enjoying and having fun with others. It is one of her pleasures as a mom.

At 8:30 a.m. she enters the office. She has time for a coffee, a few e-mails, and a chat with colleagues.

The meeting is scheduled for 9:00 a.m.

At 8:55 a.m., Katherine goes up to the second floor, where all C-levels have their offices. The COO's room is right next to the CEO's...

Katherine sees his assistant: She is busy answering morning mails. Katherine moves closer and she welcomes her unexpectedly warmly: "Good morning Katherine, I hope you have had a great weekend! They are already waiting for you. I'll show you the way."

How strange it is, she thinks: Hanna is generally colder and more distant, much less welcoming.

Alessandra and Andrew, the COO, are there, sitting and waiting for her. They welcome her and ask about the weekend. Katherine is tense: She doesn't really know what to expect.

After some pleasantries, Andrew gets to the point: "You are probably wondering why we called you here. Well, I'll get right to the point. The company is doing very well and the new strategy has proved successful. Our products are great and every day we are pleased with the feedback we receive from customers. However, to further accelerate growth, we need someone to lead our transformation and we have thought of you. Head of Digital Transformation. You would report directly to me..." While Andrew speaks, Alessandra remains silent.

Katherine is annoyed. The role they offer is not an up-leveling; it doesn't have any hierarchical advancement. It is a lateral shift: same current level, no promotion to C-level.

The role is new and she wouldn't know where to start. It is true: Every change presents an opportunity, but this is a change in an area that is completely new to her and in which she has never had an interest.

Moreover, she would leave her current boss and team for Andrew, who does not have a good reputation as a leader: He is not very innovative, has an outdated approach, and is more inclined to defend the status quo rather than to take a risk and embrace change.

Katherine knows some people in his team and all of them are unhappy with how the team is managed. Everyone is made aware only of the essentials, individuality is privileged, and there is little sharing. It is even said that Andrew organizes his monthly staff meeting once a year...

"The Head of Digital Transformation," continues Andrew, "will have to help the company transform digitally. Initially, the first project assigned to the Head of Digital Transformation will be our channel development. As you know, this area is currently of some concerns. Well, Alessandra and I would like to give you the opportunity to take this responsibility."

Indeed, Apold's channel business has been stagnating or, in fact, moving backward in the last few months. We have recently lost the "preferential partner" status with 2 of the most important European retailers and we know that the main distributor in the United States has chosen one of our competitors as a partner to launch a new, very innovative program.

Katherine is confused, a bit frightened; she doesn't know how to answer.

After a few long seconds of silence, Andrew tries to push the conversation forward: "Katherine, you don't seem enthusiastic. Look, it is a key role, quite central to our strategy. This is not the type of promotion that is offered to everyone… I'm surprised by your reaction: I would have expected more enthusiasm."

This statement has the opposite effect of the intended one. Katherine shuts away even more because she feels pressure being put on her.

Andrew continues: "This position is very important. Almost 90% of our sales come through the channel. There is a high sense of urgency to understand and redesign the dynamics of our channel programs and define a new approach. We need a capable person who is able to understand the entire spectrum of the complexity that lies ahead, rationalize it, and come up with very practical and operational solutions that we can quickly put into action."

Hum, the pressure increases. Katherine feels put in a corner and this creates some anxiety. But why her? Could this be an opportunity or is it just a way to burn her career?

Luckily, Alessandra intervenes: "I think it is a great opportunity, Katherine, both for you and the company. Don't get me wrong: You are probably the best manager in my team. Selfishly, I am not happy to let you go, but I have to put the company's interest first and offer you what I believe is a great opportunity. Why don't you sleep on it, think about it, maybe discuss it with someone you trust?

As Andrew said, the situation is urgent, but a few more days would make no difference. Think about it and let us know in the next couple of days."

The meeting ends, everyone gets up. Yes, Alessandra's proposal to take a couple of days to reflect on it sounds like a good idea.

Deep Dive—Trust

What is trust? Trust is being confident and at ease with something or someone unknown. Trust is what allows us to face the risk associated with uncertainty: It is the *bridge* between what is known and familiar (comfort zone) and what is unknown (see Figure 1.1).

Trust is a very strong glue in the relationship and interactions between executives and their collaborators. Trust in the executive creates the safe environment for collaborators to take the risk of a new challenge, expose themselves, and become vulnerable to criticism.

Trust has 2 fundamental characteristics:

- It is *specific* to a topic or a context (e.g., an executive could enjoy the trust of the team on strategic issues, but not on technological issues).
- It is *personal*, because empathy and the affinity of experience and thoughts play an important role. It also depends on the personal risk and trust inclination.

KNOWN　　　　　　　　　　　　　　　　　　　**UNKNOWN**

Figure 1.1 The bridge of trust

Credits: Sebastiano Boni

How can executives make their teams develop trust toward themselves and foster a culture based on trust within the team? Trust in a person is strengthened with:

- *Competence*: Can I show that I am competent? Do I have the experience and knowledge about a subject area?
- *Reliability*: Am I reliable? Do I have consistent behavior over time? Am I reactive in addressing a question or request about a specific topic?
- *Empathy*: Can I perceive the emotional state and needs of my employee? Do I act accordingly?
- *Integrity*: Is there alignment between my words and actions? Is there an affinity of thoughts and intentions with my collaborators?

While competence, reliability, and integrity are independent from digital reality, the virtualization of relationships and social distance affect empathy. *Digital empathy* specifically refers to the amplification of the ability to be empathic even in the absence of all the information provided by the physical presence. It will be necessary to have big ears, big eyes, and big belly to feel the needs coming from the opposite side of the net.

Trust is delicate and can break. What happens if, once built, an executive loses the trust of the employees? The consequences are serious and difficult to recover. In fact, people are impacted:

- On the *emotional level*, feeling confused and angry for having given their trust to those who did not deserve it
- At the *behavioral level*, closing, becoming defensive, less likely to take risks, and innovate

Furthermore, the loss of trust is retroactive. We ask ourselves: "But then, was it like this even before?" and we instill doubts in ourselves about the relationship and past behavior, sometimes even generalizing and extending the judgment to areas or people close to our boss.

Therefore, trust is fundamental because it consolidates relationships, allows you to face new opportunities with confidence and enables change and innovation. However, it is equally true that trust is a sensitive matter that requires ongoing attention so that it doesn't break and is strengthened over time. Time which runs fast and is the enemy of a feeling that needs confirmation to grow and develop abundantly. So, let's build it from the beginning and devote all the appropriate attention to maintain and strengthen it over time!

CHAPTER 2

Kick Off

Tuesday morning, 8:45 a.m.

Katherine decides to accept the new role: The night brought some good advice.

It will be a challenge, but a good one. Not an easy task, but it will definitely pose the opportunity to learn something new, and... it is not by facing easy things that you learn and make a career.

She communicates it to Andrew and Alessandra with a short and positive e-mail. They both reply immediately with heartfelt congratulations and announce her role immediately to the whole organization.

As her very first action, Katherine wants to meet her new team, collect their ideas and inputs to start structuring the first assignment, and at the same time establish the climate of trust and collaboration that Alessandra had been so good at creating.

Katherine is used to relying on the collective intelligence of the team and she thinks that a meeting can be an excellent opportunity to get to know each other and begin to understand their respective strengths. With this in mind, she prepares a short list of questions that she wants to use to stimulate the discussion:

- How well do you know our channel go-to market (GTM)?
- Which problems do you see in our strategy or in our execution?
- Which changes and trends do you see happening in the market?

***

Team's kick-off, 3:00 p.m.

As usual, Katherine arrives a few minutes before the start of the meeting. She finds James, one of the team members, already in the room, sitting at the table with a notepad in front of him. They already know each other by sight, but hadn't yet gotten to work together.

Shortly afterward, Mark and Maurice arrive together, each with a cup of coffee in hand. Casual and cheerful, it seems that they already know each other well and are exchanging jokes about some projects in which they were probably both involved.

Mark is in his 30s. He has been with the company for 2 years and has immediately gained a reputation as a problem solver, one who quickly understands the problem and brings a solution just as quickly. Katherine thinks he will be a valuable member of the team.

Finally, Elisabeth enters the room with a notebook and a folder full of papers. The same age as Katherine, she is there by Andrew's will. Elisabeth reported to him, in Operations, and the two really seem very similar: both very analytical, little creative, and reluctant to change.

Katherine suspects that Andrew might have selected Elisabeth for the team as his way of controlling her, but she does not want to start with bad thoughts and tries to ignore them.

After a brief round of introductions, Katherine introduces the subject: "Dear Team, I would have preferred to have more time to get to know each other, maybe start with a real kick-off meeting off-site, but unfortunately we have to postpone it. The leadership team has assigned us an urgent project."

"I guess it has to do with the problems we have with the channel," Elisabeth intervenes. "Andrew mentioned it to me a few days ago... and so I have done some analysis. In fact, I have prepared some slides. If you pass me the projector cable, I'll show you right away."

An interesting start, thinks Katherine. She is blown away by Elisabeth's debut, who seems to want to lead the meeting. However, she decides not to interject, rather put the best face on a slippery situation, and remain as open-minded as possible.

Elisabeth continues: "I have analyzed all our channel data from the last 3 years, in terms of both turnover and profit. I have divided them by geographical areas, products sold, and types of resellers, separating distributors from resellers, as per our corporate taxonomy. I was only able to work on it for a few days, but in my opinion, it is quite evident that the program we are already implementing addresses all the important priorities, namely (1) priority to strategic products with the highest margin, (2) focus on resellers with the highest sales volumes, (3) opportunistic management of the rest."

"Elisabeth, this is very interesting," Mark intervenes. "It really seems an excellent analysis to me. Have you also talked to any resellers?"

"Oh, no, with no one. I didn't have the time, but I think there is no need: We literally have a sea of data that we can use, we know everything about our sales, and we can follow every single product from the moment it leaves the factory to the moment it arrives on the shelves of our resellers. We have everything we need! In my opinion, and I know that Andrew agrees because I spoke to him last night, we need to deepen the plan we already made, update it with the figures from the last quarter, review the schedule of activities, and above all be more assertive in the way we communicate it to our channel partners."

Katherine thinks to Einstein's famous line that "Insanity is doing the same thing over and over again and expecting different results" and she can't hold back a smile… She chooses not to comment and prefers a different approach: "Elisabeth, thank you very much, it's all very interesting. I appreciate that you are so proactive and started looking into the problem before we even met. Very useful… Now I'd like to hear what others think about it. James? Maurice?"

Although not asked, it is Mark who intervenes: "I believe that Elisabeth's analysis is important, but it is only one side of the coin: ours. We absolutely must also look at the other one, which is the market, the customers, and, in this case, the channel. Our numbers are important, but our business is people-to-people rather than business-to-business. If we have a problem with some resellers, the first thing is to visit them, speak with them, and try to understand their point of view."

Elisabeth replies with a certain hastiness: "Mark, as Andrew said, there is a certain urgency: We must find a solution quickly. You propose to meet the resellers with whom, among other things, we wouldn't even know what to talk about… none of us have a specific channel background and we certainly don't have the time to build it now. Here we just need to divide the roles: I can analyze the correlation between sales and margin, you and Maurice can verify how the channel program is aligned with the business strategy, and James can design a new dashboard to report the results. We give each other a few weeks and then we meet to put together the various pieces into a single proposal that we can present to Andrew."

Mark, a little annoyed, continues: "True Elisabeth, Maurice, and I come from the Product division, you are from Operations, James from Finance, and Katherine has a Marketing background: None of us come from the Channel. But this could also be our strength: The diversity and mix of skills of our team lead us to be free from preconceptions. We can see the problem from different perspectives."

Maurice intervenes, supporting Mark's point: "In my opinion Mark is right. I think we must at least explore other options before assuming that we only need to delve into the current model."

"Additionally," adds Mark, "this does not necessarily take a long time: We are a small team and we can move with agility, operating in an iterative way."

Katherine agrees with Mark, but she does not want to take a too clear stance toward Elisabeth's proposal. She has been very clear about her link with Andrew and it seems that for both of them "the solution is obvious."

"Well," Elisabeth concludes, "it has been a very interesting first meeting and I thank everyone for your contribution. We are at a key point: The approach we choose will affect the development of the project and therefore its success. Let's pause here, let's give some more thoughts to our options, and reconvene tomorrow at 9:00 to make a decision with lucidity."

As they leave the room, Katherine thinks of James: He didn't contribute anything, he didn't take a stand, he didn't share any information. He was a stranger to the dynamics of the meeting; he looked more like a spectator than a team member.

I will have to figure out how to get him involved. I need everyone's strength and expertise for this project.

Now, however, Katherine wants to update Alessandra and ask her for advice.

She is at the desk in the daily routine of checking e-mails. She is happy to see her and Katherine tells Alessandra about the kick-off meeting and the team's disagreement. "The team is divided. Some are for a traditional approach: They want to tune the current model and they propose that everyone work in parallel on individual tasks. Others would like to engage with the resellers, identify alternative channel models, converge on a viable idea, and test it as soon as possible. They propose that we work as a team and leverage our diversity. What do you think?"

Alessandra smiles: "I'm happy to tell you, but first tell me what you think and if you have a preference."

"Well, the second way seems more innovative to me and I'm sure it can lead to a better result, but it also seems riskier. It is more difficult to explain to our stakeholders, especially for such a big and important project."

"I think you are right... Sure you might find it difficult with some more conservative stakeholders, but we proposed you for this role precisely so that you can change things, so don't be too afraid. The approach that you define as the most innovative is close to what is called Design Thinking. I can give you a good article about it."

"The preference between one approach or the other," continues Alessandra, "depends on your propensity to find innovative solutions, outside the box and the traditional logic. In a changing and unstable business context like ours, it is definitely worth to question the old assumptions, consider more hypotheses, experiment, and try."

"A phrase I read somewhere comes to mind: 'It is very difficult to make predictions, especially about the future.'"

Alessandra smiles: "You have to take some risks and accept the failure as an opportunity to experiment and improve. Design Thinking is an iterative process and it is the most suitable if you want to innovate."

"Thanks, Alessandra: This chat was very useful to me. Send me the article you said, please. I will read it tonight and tomorrow I will present my decision to the team. Thanks again."

Deep Dive—Design Thinking

Among the most cited concepts today, Design Thinking is a set of interconnected principles used to solve a wider and wider range of problems. It was born with the aim of exploring new perspectives and identifying the best emotional and functional idea to solve a problem. Typically associated with innovation, its applicability is much more extensive. What are the fundamental principles of Design Thinking?

- *Human centricity*: People (customers, partners, employees, citizens, and so on) are the heart of Design Thinking. The observation of habits and needs, the generation of ideas, the prototyping, finetuning, and implementation of the solution revolve around them. Potential customers become cocreators of the winning idea: The designers emphatically engage and collaborate with them and they guide the team toward the final solution.
- *Small data*: The more generic and impersonal market trends are complemented by small data—habits, uses, behaviors—which become generators of new creative ideas. Design Thinking recognizes consumers with extreme behaviors or needs as the best source of inspiration.

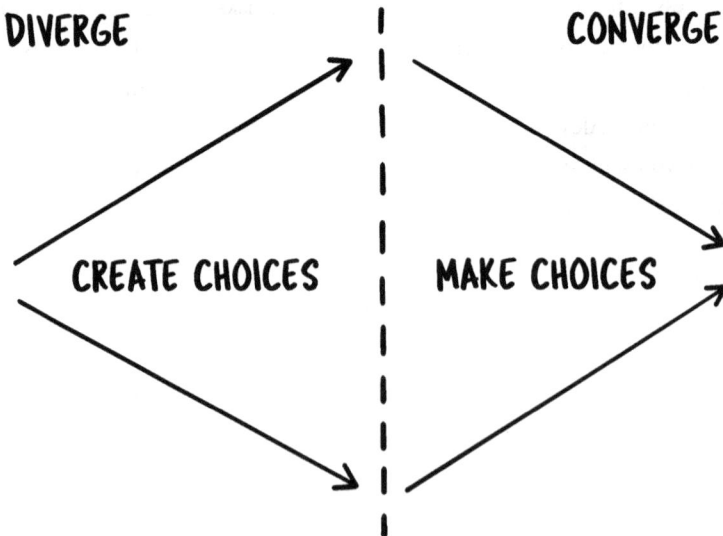

DIVERGE   **CONVERGE**

CREATE CHOICES   **MAKE CHOICES**

Figure 2.1 The diamond of Design Thinking

Credits: Sebastiano Boni

- *Divergence–convergence*: As illustrated in Figure 2.1, Design Thinking finds the answer to a problem after creating and evaluating multiple options. More options mean more chances of finding the best alternative for customers. Once having explored different alternatives, it is necessary to discard some of them and converge toward those that simultaneously meet the criteria of:
  - ○ Customer desirability
  - ○ Business and financial viability
  - ○ Technical feasibility
- *Interdisciplinarity of the team*: Key for the generalization of ideas is the coexistence of different skills in the design team. As suggested by McKinsey & Company, the best profile of every team player is T-shaped: They must be a deep expert of a topic (e.g., visual design) and have curiosity and constant exposure to other topics. This allows them to understand and contribute to apparently lateral issues to their core competence. Then, Design Thinking rewards the influence of experiences in favor of the greater creativity of the entire team.
- *Prototype*: A key role in Design Thinking is played by the prototype, that is, the tangible representation of the idea (or sometimes multiple ideas) considered to be the best option. The prototypes allow you to see and touch the idea, telling it better. Depending on the designed object, the prototype can be made in different ways (e.g., storyboard, video, application screens, physical object). The prototype is aimed to get feedback on the idea and to understand if and how to proceed with the roll-out activities. Therefore, it's better to make the prototype as soon as possible to eventually correct the course of the following activities.
- *Critical thinking*: Constantly asking the question "why?" allows the team to question assumptions and encourages reflection on the conditions taken for granted/acquired. Then, critical thinking drives creativity.
- *Experimentation and freedom to mistake*: In Design Thinking it is allowed to make mistakes as long as this happens at the beginning of the process and is the way to learn for the team.

What is the Design Thinking process? Although similar, there are several Design Thinking processes. IDEO, which is acknowledged for the birth of the term *Design Thinking* and its application to any business area, reports a process made up of 3 interconnected and iterative phases:

- *Inspiration*: The first phase is dedicated to understanding the problem and gathering the information necessary to generate insights. Typically, it starts with a *brief*, which includes the macro constraints and information needed to understand the problem, objectives, and expected results. Once you understand the *what*, this phase involves the collection of information through various types of research.
- *Concept*: The second phase is dedicated to the generation, development, and testing of ideas. Creativity and intuition drive the generation of ideas; the best ideas are selected, prototyped, and tested to collect feedback internally and externally in the market and then finetuned, reiterating the process until the best idea is defined.
- *Implementation*: The last phase is dedicated to bringing the idea to the market, defining and implementing a launch plan.

The typical criticism made about Design Thinking is that of being a too iterative and inefficient process. However, many modern projects are canceled exactly because the initial idea is not solid and differentiating. Therefore, it's more convenient for a company to spend more time in the conceptualization of the winning idea through a Design Thinking process than investing a significant budget in projects without a solid idea behind.

CHAPTER 3

Let's Go!

Wednesday, 9:00 a.m.

Everyone is on time and ready to start the meeting. By now Katherine is sure of the direction to take: She is convinced that Design Thinking is the best approach and Alessandra's encouragement in this direction has given her a lot of confidence.

She does not want to impose herself on the team: She prefers to try to bring everyone on board by convincing them of the approach.

Elisabeth had been a bit annoying the day before, with constant references to Andrew and their conversations, but she certainly invested time in preparation and analysis. This cannot be denied.

"Good morning!" Katherine begins. "First of all thanks again for yesterday's discussion. We had different opinions, but it was a positive and productive conversation. A constructive discussion between us will always be fundamental to evaluate the range of possible options and choose the path that we will decide is the best for the company."

"True, Katherine, but we must also make a decision," Elisabeth immediately intervenes. "The debate itself can be fascinating, but we also have to produce results and there is a lot of work to cover."

Katherine is a little surprised by what seems a personal attack, but she decides not to be discouraged. Vice versa, she goes to the whiteboard and picks up a marker: "Absolutely, yes, and I thank you for this point, Elisabeth. So let's try to rationalize yesterday's discussion and see if we agree on what characterizes the current situation before deciding which approach we want to take. Let's start. Elisabeth, would you say that the problem we have to face, I mean the channel market, is stable or has it changed a lot in recent years?"

"Obviously it has changed a lot, we all know it," Elisabeth answers a little ironically.

Katherine writes the first line at the top of the board: "Market under significant changes."

"Maurice, as far as we know, based on what was discussed yesterday, and given that the market context is of 'significant changes,' how likely is it that the solution requires an innovative approach or vice versa the optimization of the current approach?"

"It seems obvious to me: The market scenario is very different from what we knew only a couple of years ago and it is still evolving so it is likely that a new approach could be beneficial to us," replies Maurice.

"Are we all on the same page? Anyone has a different opinion?" asks Katherine as she turns to the whiteboard and adds 2 new lines: "Fast evolving context" and "Need for a new model."

Katherine pauses for a few seconds to let everyone internalize the points and possibly chime in. After a few moments, everyone nods, then she continues: "What do we think of the data? Should we analyze all the available market reports and our own internal data on turnover and profit trends... or should we complement them with direct interviews with channel operators and perhaps their customers, to gain a first-hand understanding of their behaviors, purchase criteria, preferences, and so on?"

"The latter," Mark immediately jumps in. "We need a mix of big data and small data."

Katherine writes "small AND big data" on the whiteboard.

"Well, Team. According to an article, I read last night, we have just described the almost complete list of reasons why a Design Thinking style approach is preferable."

So saying, Katherine distributes to everyone 2 photocopied pages of the article which include a table almost identical to what is written on the whiteboard.

The approach is chosen. Everyone seems convinced and the second part of the meeting is much more fluid and operational. They decide which partners and customers to interview, how best to open the conversation with them, how to avoid introducing any bias, the questions to ask, partly open and partly closed.

The energy level in the room also feels better. Except for James who once again remains on the sidelines. Katherine had thought of involving him, asking him a direct question, but then she preferred to turn to Maurice because it would have been difficult for her to manage a silence while trying to build consensus and energy.

The meeting quickly comes to define a good action plan and they decide to reupdate the following morning.

As everyone leaves the room, Katherine calls James.

"James, sorry, do you have a moment? There is one aspect on which I would need your help. Can we go to lunch together and talk about it?"

"Yes, of course, Katherine, tell me what time you prefer," James kindly replies.

***

Apold's canteen, 12:30 p.m.

They choose a table a little apart from the others to be able to converse more privately. Katherine is undecided on how to enter the subject without putting James on the defensive and aggravating his disengagement.

"James, I would like to know what you think about the project because I noticed that you didn't intervene much during our first meetings. I know your background and I'm sure you have an opinion."

"What they have assigned to us is certainly a real problem that must be addressed. The channel situation is not pretty when you look at the numbers. I also think that the senior leadership team made the right decision in creating a dedicated new team with a new leader, someone who doesn't carry too much baggage for considering a real transformation. It might have not been the most obvious choice; I'm sure several C-levels would have liked to put their name on the project."

"Yes, you are probably right, but... what do you think? Are we taking the right direction?"

"Yes, I think so. I am not an expert in Design Thinking, but I too have read a couple of articles on the subject. Indeed I have also followed some short webinars, but then I thought it was not a good use of my time because it seems to me that here the corporate culture is almost the opposite."

"Do you speak from experience? I mean, have you made Design Thinking proposals that have been turned down?" continues Katherine, starting to understand the problem.

"Frankly no, I lacked the energy. Or rather... the context, in which I was in, was discouraging. You see, I believe that innovation is the key to success in our market, but it seems to me that the company rewards only the most conservative behaviors. So, I correct myself, yes: I tried, in the past, but after bumping into roadblocks a couple of times, I realized that it was better to let it go and that my point of view was not particularly appreciated by my leadership."

Katherine goes further: "Do you know the story of the 2 stonecutters?"

"No... I don't think so."

"A pilgrim visiting a big city sees a worker who is cutting stones and he asks him what he is doing. He replies: 'Can't you see it? I break stones from morning to night: a terrible job, it's hot here under the sun, it's dusty, I break my back for 2 pennies.' The pilgrim understands that it is not wise to continue the conversation. Then he sees another worker nearby, apparently intent on the same job, but all smiling. The pilgrim approaches him and asks him the same question: 'What are you doing, good man?' and this: 'I do the greatest job in the world! I'm building the Cathedral!'"

"I understand Katherine. You are telling me that I feel like the first worker, but it's up to me to see the Cathedral."

"And chime in, please. I would be very grateful, James, if you could. We need everyone here; indeed, the more we manage to put together different points of view, the more this will affect the quality of the outcome."

"Ok, Katherine, I'll try... I promise... meanwhile I tell you that you are the first manager in many years who talks to me in this way and I thank you for this. It's encouraging and I'm happy to be part of the team."

Katherine is a little more relieved: Perhaps she has brought James back to the team. We will see it in the next few days.

Now everything seems set: The approach is decided, and the team is engaged. But will the team be able to make progress? This remains to be seen: It is a new team, with balance and teamwork still to be tested.

Deep Dive—Purpose

What does it make you get up every morning and go to work? What motivates you?

Money, career, duty are the most frequent answers. Personal fulfillment is, unfortunately, a very rare one.

Purpose is the meaning, the inner force which motives us every single day, the reason why we exist.

Purpose grows in the personal sphere and corresponds to our ultimate realization, the reason that drives us to our self, to the contribution we want to leave in this world (e.g., for an executive, the purpose could be to contribute to the discovery and maximization of the potential of their collaborators). Linked to the purpose are the identity (e.g., an executive could recognize oneself as a mentor/coach) and the values that guide us (e.g., altruism, help, integrity).

Purpose, identity, and values are personal aspects that everyone should analyze and be aware of. This allows us to feel fulfilled and avoid or resolve the crisis, which arises when we move away from our deepest selves (see Figure 3.1).

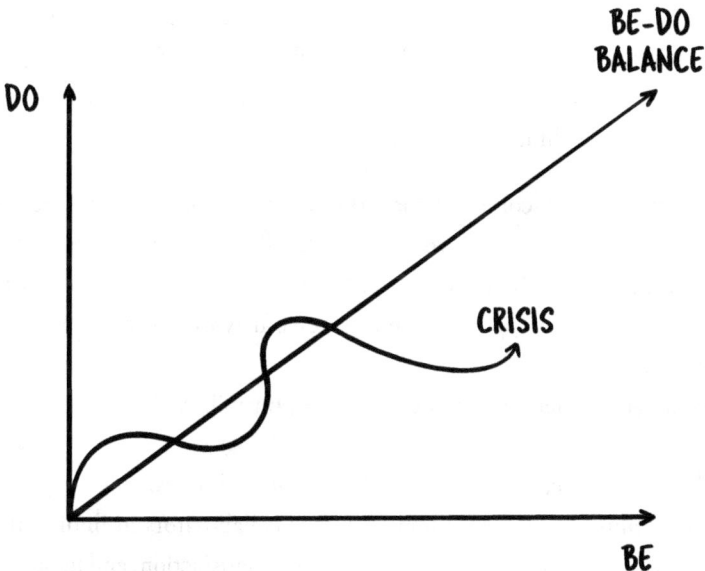

Figure 3.1 The human being trade-off

Credits: Sebastiano Boni

After the enthusiasm of the early working years, people very often find themselves in a vicious circle, overwhelmed by activities and duty (the *doing*), and they lose the sight of the meaning of what they do. Without a meaning, frustration, tiredness, disengagement sometimes take over. When this happens, people fall apart—they do not recognize themselves in what they do and feel as if they are sacrificing their life without a reason.

Purpose is missed. Meaning is missed. Individual values are missed.

It is not necessary to change jobs to rebalance *doing* and *being*, but it is key to reinterpret or adapt the job so that it is clear how this can align to and express our purpose and values. Therefore:

- *Importance*: What is important to you? What gives or would make sense of your working days? What are your values?
- *Coherence and affiliation*: Think about the corporate strategy and culture—How is it consistent with your purpose and values? Do you feel part of a bigger project?
- *Alignment*: Analyze the projects you are working on. What can you do to make small changes to the way you work so that it is more aligned with your values? What energizes and engages you?
- *Sharing*: Reflect on colleagues. Who shares your same values? Who do you love to work with and relate to? With whom can you build a solid and functional relationship to create a better working climate?

There won't be a company that 100% reflects your needs, but each will have aspects aligned with you. Identify them! Nothing is more motivating than an inner voice. Neither corporate mission nor salary nor career incentive can spur you and make your work meaningful as your purpose.

Personal fulfillment is an individual responsibility. Seek it, create it, reach it!

As an executive, you will have a second, but equally important responsibility: helping or supporting your collaborators in finding their own purpose. This will allow their fulfillment, satisfaction, and happiness, with the consequent increase in motivation, dedication, and creativity with direct benefit in productivity and engagement (see Figure 3.2).

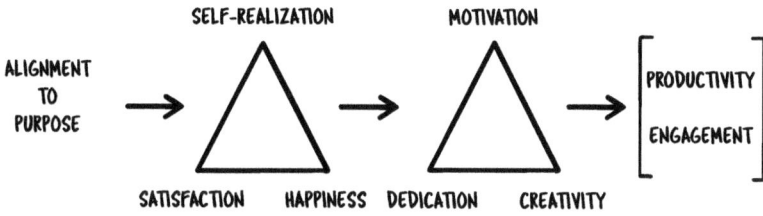

Figure 3.2 The purpose value chain

Credits: Sebastiano Boni

CHAPTER 4

The Following Morning

Thursday, 9:00 a.m.

The team is back together again. It is Mark who opens the discussion, without being invited to do so. "Perfect," thinks Katherine, "Mark proves to be an excellent ally."

"Yesterday was an excellent day. James and I spoke to 2 dealers, one from Sweden and one from the United Kingdom, and they gave us some very interesting points of view."

"Yes," adds James, who finally intervenes in the discussion. "In particular, the UK one told us that most of their sales are now through e-commerce. This is quite obvious, but the less apparent insight is that this has led to change in the criteria they use to give visibility to the different products in the catalog and that this could have created some disadvantage for us."

"Well, I don't think we should give too much weight to a couple of opinions, without even a single piece of information supporting them," Elisabeth interrupts abruptly. "Our channel is made up of several thousand resellers. We cannot be misled by a single opinion and we certainly cannot speak to hundreds of resellers. Not within the tight deadlines of this project."

"Of course not," says Mark, "but maybe a hundred yes. We are 5, counting Katherine. If each of us talks to 4 retailers a day, in a week it is 5 of us by 4 retailers times 5 days: just a 100..."

"Mark, are you suggesting that we turn ourselves into a sort of call center?" Elisabeth replies with disdain, "and then sorry, 100 is better than 2, but do you know how many things we could learn from analyzing the numbers we already have in our hands? And our numbers are the result of the sales of all our resellers, not just a hundred of them."

It seems that Elisabeth is firm on her beliefs and she tries to dampen the enthusiasm of the rest of the team. James intervenes again: "Elisabeth, I would not look at the 2 approaches as alternatives. On the contrary,

I think that direct interviews can provide us with the human side of our retailers and end customers, how they position our products, and how they make decisions. These insights would enable us to better interpret the numbers we have."

It's Maurice's turn: "I tend to line with James: This is information that we cannot take from any market reports, no matter how much we squeeze them. And anyway it is a complementary view to the data, not a substitute, Elisabeth."

"Guys, sorry," Elisabeth insists, "I would like to remind you that we are the ones who train the channel on new trends and educate them on how purchasing behaviors change."

"True, Elisabeth," Maurice continues, "but you know very well that everything we say is to bring water to our mill. In our training, we talk about ourselves, our new products, and what comes out of our Research and Development rather than the real needs of our customers."

"Okay, how is it then that the major market research houses ask us for trends and then rewrite them, embellished, in the reports that make us pay an arm and a leg? Maybe we are not so ignorant of what happens in the market, don't you think? We have to go deeper, not broaden the field," concludes Elisabeth.

"Elisabeth," James is speaking again, "you may be right, but you too will agree that talking to retailers and customers cannot do any harm... provided that we are open-minded, not trying to validate our biases or assuming they will not tell us anything interesting."

After leaving the team debating for a good half hour, Katherine decides it is time to converge on a final decision: "It seems to me that most of us are to interview the resellers, but Elisabeth's points are also valid. We are a leader in our sector and the leaders are known for their ability to listen and grasp even the weak signals, so, I find the proposal to listen to some retailers very interesting." Then turning to Elisabeth, but always speaking to everyone: "Precisely because we are leaders we should not be afraid to learn. On the contrary, we need to be open to different perspectives and continue learning from the market."

After a moment of silence, Mark comes forward: "If you like, after the first 2 interviews with James, I have put down a short list of questions. The first ones are open questions to put us in listening mode without influencing the reseller; the following questions are closed, to validate some specific points. If we all used the same track, it will then be easier to compare the results."

"It's a great idea, thanks, Mark." Katherine replies: "The worst risk we can run is to confirm what we already know. As an upside, however, we can learn new information and collect good ideas for our project. Once we will have our sweep of the horizon done, we will follow Elisabeth's guidance to deepen our findings and make sure we have facts and data supporting them."

The use of Elisabeth's direct quote softens the atmosphere a little and many smile or nod. Elisabeth, on the other hand, remains impassive: She does not seem to have appreciated the open recognition of her analytical skills.

All in all, it was a good meeting. Katherine is not afraid of animated discussions, as long as everyone can contribute, each with their own strengths.

***

11:30 a.m.

Katherine goes to Elisabeth's desk. She is busy in a phone conversation, but she seems to be about to finish it, so Katherine signals that she has no rush. Elisabeth puts it down shortly after, turns to Katherine, and tells her: "He was our main reseller for France. He was very courteous and above all confirmed my points. Even with them, we are losing market share, albeit not dramatically. He confirmed to me that every week they send us all the sales and inventory numbers and he is sure that all the other resellers do the same as well. His conclusion was: 'You already have everything to solve the problem.' Then he told me that if he wants we can talk about it, but he doesn't understand how he can help us."

"Did you follow Mark's list of open questions?"

"Frankly no, it seems to me that it makes us waste time. I preferred to go straight to the point."

"I know we would all like to arrive as quickly as possible to identify the initiatives that we should develop..."

"So why don't we start eliminating this extra work that we frankly created ourselves?"

"You are very performance oriented, Elisabeth, and your deep technical and analytical skills strengthen you in this. But sometimes it makes sense to balance performance with listening and learning. Trust and listen to different points of view."

"Yes, it's true, Katherine, I am driven by performance. When I work on a project, I aim at the target and I try to reach it as soon as possible. It seemed to me that the way to go was clear, but I see that you prefer to follow Mark's ideas..."

"I think that your technical competence and the desire for perfection sometimes make you..." Katherine hesitates.

"You can say that. They make me look inflexible. However, these are the same traits that other people call rigor and attention to detail. Sorry, I need to make another call now. If it's important, I can come to you later."

"No, I'll leave you to your work Elisabeth. Just know that you can count on me if you want."

In the end, technical skills are important, but they are not enough. Attitude makes the difference. Katherine is happy to have seen James participate in the discussion, but she is worried that Elisabeth has felt put in a corner.

Back at her desk, Katherine finds a Post-it from Andrew that says: "Are you making progress??" It could be a simple request for an update from the boss, but the double question mark makes her a little nervous.

Deep Dive—Performance, Interferences, and Mindset

What is performance? How can we maximize it?
Gallwey's[1] equation considers:

$$Performance = Potential - Interferences$$

Performance is equal to the potential net of the interferences which decrease its effectiveness. To maximize performance, it's necessary to avoid or limit every type of interference. Interferences can be internal beliefs (e.g., the inability to do a certain thing) or external situations (e.g., organizational change). Typically, they generate:

- An interior dialogue, which judges, criticizes, paralyzes
- An emotional reaction (e.g., feeling of anxiety)
- A physiological reaction (e.g., sweaty hands, contracted muscles)

How is it possible to manage interferences, maximizing performance and limiting the impacts they create?
The best way is to change perspective, shifting focus from performance to *enjoyment* and *learning* (*learn culture*). The achievement of a performance goal, therefore, becomes the consequence and not the primary goal. In this way, attention is diverted from the performance goal and limits the inner dialogue that knocks it down.
We move from a *fixed mindset*, focused on achieving a fixed, preset goal, to a *growth mindset*, in which difficulties, mistakes, and setbacks are a natural part of a learning journey (see Figure 4.1).
Changing perspective means changing mindset. It means considering difficulties and mistakes as *opportunities* for growth. It means identifying the *process* and the *strategies* for dealing with difficulties, consolidating

---

[1] W. Timothy Gallwey is a coach and the author of the best-seller "The inner game of tennis." His work has often been credited as the foundation of the new fields of business and life coaching. As a boy, he was a nationally ranked tennis player in his division and later captained his Harvard University team.

and reusing them if the same difficulties arise again. How does it work? It is necessary to:

- *Increase mindfulness*, learn how to recognize *fixed minded behaviors*, and *analyze difficulties and interferences*,
  ○ Verifying and describing the causes and, possibly, recognizing the situations triggering the fixed mindset behaviors and the weakening internal dialogue
  ○ Identifying its characteristics
  ○ Highlighting the impacts (physical, emotional, cognitive)

  For example, suppose you feel insecure speaking French and, whenever the need arises, an internal voice belittles you and reminds you of episodes in which your performance was not the best. Ask yourself: "Am I really weak in French? What is the concrete evidence that proves my inability? When does it occur? How? What impact does it have?"

- *Uncouple and distance the interference from our identity.*
  An effective trick to put distance between the interference and ourselves is to associate it with another self, giving it a name. This allows us to give it a separate identity, see and treat it at a distance, with greater rationality and less involvement, thus limiting its ability to influence us negatively.

  Continuing the previous example, the internal voice can be attributed to a self, which you could call with any invention name (e.g., *X*) and which is revealed in the ways previously analyzed. *X* has its own identity, external and separate from yours.

- *Recognize and codify the strategies* previously adopted or that can be adopted whenever the other-self manifests itself and attempts to bring down our performance. Continuing the example, what have you done in the past or what can you do to contain or reduce the impact of *X*? For example, you can get better prepared; you can reflect on the message, expected questions, and possible answers; you can look for any unfamiliar terms; and so on.

- Have *confidence* in our abilities and *reuse the strategies* identified previously to face the most difficult challenges. To end the example, whenever the conditions that anticipate the arrival of *X* are recognized, you will apply the same winning strategies that have worked in the past. New successes will help you gain trust and activate a virtuous circle of self-confidence and better performance.

In the digital age in which activities and relationships are increasingly virtual, interferences to our performance are amplified by the fluid, dynamic, uncertain working environment. The pressure and the search for ever better performances generate stress, sleep disorders, sometimes burnout. We give up our needs and lose our balance (notably, homeostasis). The right mindset is key to live the contemporary reality, reinterpreting pressure as a challenge to be faced with joy and lucidity as an opportunity for growth and learning. The executive will have an important mission— to adopt and transfer the right mindset to his entire team, preventing the pressure from impacting their performance or, worse, their health.

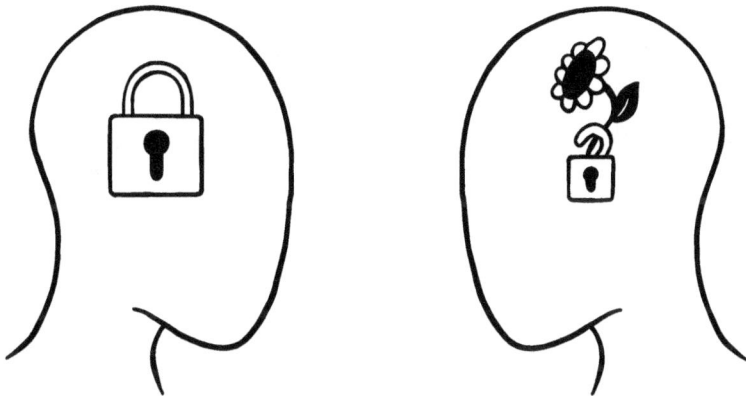

Figure 4.1 Fixed and growth mindset

Credits: Sebastiano Boni

CHAPTER 5

Tennis Class

After seeing Andrew's Post-it note, Katherine prefers to take a break and have a coffee rather than respond immediately.

In the coffee area, she meets Mary, the head of Human Resources. Katherine is happy: Mary is one of her closest friends. In her 40s, small constitution, large glasses covering half her face. She has a vocation for her work and, when she can help people, she lights up, smiling with motherly eyes.

They are alone at the coffee machine and Katherine takes the opportunity to steal advice from her: "Mary, are you in a hurry? May I ask you for advice?"

"Of course. By the way, I have not yet congratulated you on your new assignment: well done, wow! An excellent step and a very well deserved one."

"Thank you, Mary, but I am not so sure there is anything to congratulate about. In fact, I would like to talk to you about my new role or rather ask your advice about some challenges that I am finding in engaging with my new team."

In short, Katherine sums up the situation: She tells of Elisabeth's hostile or at least uncooperative attitude, of Andrew's pressure, and of the Post-it note that she is unsure on how to interpret.

Mary listens, without interrupting, and, when Katherine has finished, she smiles at her and says: "I renew my congratulations because in a few days you got started, you brought the team together, you chose an approach, you are diagnosing some possible dysfunctions, and you are already taking care of improving teamwork and everyone's involvement. I'll tell you what I think separates a senior person like you from others who, despite maybe a fancy job title or age, do not have the same level of maturity and therefore of effectiveness in achieving results."

"Tell me: I'm all ears."

"The secret is attitude..." Mary pauses to allow Katherine time to absorb her words, then she continues: "I mean how a person confronts situations, whether they are problems or opportunities. It is the mix of skills and attitude that determines success. Attitude is what brings out competence, what allows you to continue and progress even in periods of uncertainty, build support around your ideas, motivating and guiding others to follow you. People prefer to follow those who have a positive vision but are also able to raise the right questions, as long as they do so in the right way and at the right time, with curiosity, without accusations or judgment."

"I understand what you are saying. With Andrew I find it hard to understand if he is looking for a culprit or if he is really trying to understand the issue, go to the bottom of the possible causes, and, ultimately, help ... which certainly does not put me in the most comfortable position to give my best."

"Sure. Leaders must know how to adapt their approach. Depending on who is in front of them, they must be able to motivate, support, or simply be silent and in the background. What if we were all more aware of our emotional state and the one we create in others? What would we achieve if we could always tune our attitude and language to the situation? Here, this is one of the traits of what I have called attitude."

Katherine nods and she thinks that emotional intelligence is not one of Andrew's strengths. Could she, however, try to reach out to him using her emotional intelligence and bring forth Andrew's true intention, going beyond the literal meaning of his messages?

"Let me add one more thing, Katherine. Perhaps the most important element in what I have called attitude is antifragility. Knowing yourself well, both at work and outside, this is one of your strengths."

"Do you mean that I do not bend or break?" smiles Katherine.

"On the contrary, antifragility is being able to bend without breaking, combined with foreseeing and taking new opportunities. It is a bit like those toy puppets that always come back to a straight position after rotating on their base to find a new, better balance.

It is not stubbornness. Antifragility means knowing how to learn from mistakes, get up from falls, and not keep bumping your head against the same wall."

"I get it. What you call attitude is a mix of various elements and above all the ability to balance them... Mary, as usual, talking to you is great: You have cheered me up and encouraged me."

Katherine looks at her watch: If she hurries, she may still have time to pick up Luke from tennis. She hasn't seen him play in a long time and he would be delighted. It is also important to know how to keep work and personal life in harmony.

"Mary, thank you! Now I have to run. I have some things that I want to finish and then I would like to try to get out a little earlier and pick up Luke from tennis."

"Good idea. See you soon. Say hello to Luke and Thomas too."

Katherine manages to close all the most urgent items and arrives at the Tennis Club just before the end of the lesson. Luke is very passionate about tennis and he has made excellent progress in the last year, so much so that he joined the Tennis Club competitive team. At first, Katherine was doubtful: She was afraid that tennis could go from fun to duty and become a source of stress for a small child.

But she had to change her mind. The relationship between Luke and his coach became immediately of great respect and Katherine is sure that this is one of the reasons why she saw Luke maturing a lot in the last few months. Now they are preparing for their first tournament.

Approaching the court, Katherine does not hear the classic noise of the balls against the strings of the rackets. There is silence on the pitch: Have they finished earlier today?

Katherine comes closer and she sees the coach who has called the children together: There are 4 today and he is talking to them: "Tennis is a sport of technique and mind. You are all making progress on technique. We still have a long way to go, new hits to put in your arsenal, and above all to practice. A lot of work, but let me ask you a simple question: Do you enjoy playing tennis?"

The coach looks at them one by one and all the boys nod, one shouts "very much!" and the coach gives him a high five with a snap, which echoes inside the tennis dome.

"But, guys, the technique is not enough to become champions. It is the head that makes the difference. Of course, you have to train and improve your technique, but usually, it's not the player with the best technique who wins."

The boys seem doubtful.

"It is the mix between technique and attitude that determines success!"

Katherine gasps: These are the same words that Mary used with her a few hours earlier. Now Katherine listens with even more attention: "Just see that I have more to learn than Luke here."

The coach continues: "It is the mental training that helps you manage emotions, play naturally, and take control of the game. That's where you can take advantage of the weaknesses of your opponent, slow down, or speed up the pace to create stress for the other player. Adapt to the situation to always show confidence."

"Will you teach us also about these things?" asks Luke.

"Not me. But you are right, Luke, we must exercise our minds also and soon you will start meetings with mental coaches. I will continue to train you on the pitch. With me, you will work to improve your technique and physical endurance, with the other coach you will learn to manage how you feel, to keep yourself motivated, not to be discouraged by a ball in the net, but rather to show your opponent that you are stronger, even when technically it may not be the case. Enough for today, guys, we have finished the hour and I see that some of your parents are already here. Go! Everyone to the locker room and I'll see you on Thursday! Goodbye."

While waiting for Luke to finish the shower, Katherine thinks: "Two attitude lessons in the same afternoon. Let's see if now I'll be able to put them into practice in the review with Andrew next Monday."

Deep Dive—Attitude

COVID-19 has made us more digital than ever. We had to react quickly, interpret change as a challenge, think differently, and periodically reflect on what drives and motivates us. Social relationships have become virtual; interpersonal interaction has been limited and replaced by loneliness and discomfort. The new reality has emphasized the need to possess 5 already important, but now necessary skills helping to read opportunities in change and respond to difficulty and uncertainty with positivity and mind openness. These 5 skills are:

- *Positivity*: It is key to constructively and productively focus our energies on embracing new opportunities. Positivity is linked to our awareness of purpose and personal inclination to antifragility. Being positive (as well as being negative) is contagious: The executive's positivity will strengthen the team's confidence about the future.
- *Antifragility*: It is *resilience 2.0* because it not only allows us to adapt and cope with the unexpected, but also to interpret change as an opportunity, stimulate alternative ideas, experiment, and get benefits (see Figure 5.1).

  Are antifragile people change-insensitive? Or do they experience the same difficulties, doubts, and fatigue as all others when change happens? Of course, they do. We all struggle when handling new things. However, the antifragile people have the ability to accept novelty (as part of their life and growth) and reframe current facts and situations within a wider context, in which there are always winning strategies to deal with difficulties and achieve objectives. We call *storytelling* the ability to tell the right story, reinterpreting facts, editing the narrative, motivating the protagonist to achieve the goal. Storytelling allows us to be the *author* of our life and see the story from outside, changing it if necessary, contextualizing and rereading facts in a broader context. Storytelling gives the distance to facts and helps designing future actions with clarity and rationality.

Figure 5.1 Antifragility: Adapt and take new opportunities

Credits: Sebastiano Boni

- *Creativity*: It is necessary to find solutions to previously non-existent problems. Creativity is the result of the connection or the implication of well-known, existing solutions. It is stimulated by curiosity, careful observation (*mindfulness*), and exposure to different topics. The creative idea typically arises when the brain is in default mode (notably, DMN—*default mode network*), defocused and only apparently at rest. At that moment, apparently calm, the brain is active and engaged in significant brain activities. Therefore, there is no need to restlessly focus on finding a solution. On the opposite, it is useful to leave the brain the time and space to find its answers and avoid forcing it to look for a solution at all costs.

- *Critical thinking*: It is important because it questions beliefs, personal prejudices, and the status quo and opens alternative and useful scenarios to find the best solution in new and uncertain times. Critical thinking is fueled by questions:
  - Why?
  - What else?

  It should be promoted at all levels of the organization and applied bidirectionally between executives and collaborators.
- *Emotional intelligence (EI)*: It is needed for managing emotions related to uncertainty and change.

  EI is the sensitivity and the ability to recognize our own emotions and those of others to manage them effectively. It is a mix of 5 components: self-awareness, self-regulation, motivation, empathy, social skills. The first 2 are important for recognizing and/or controlling our emotions, the last 3 play an important role in the relationship with others. Interpreting others' needs allows us to effectively relate with them, calibrate our communication, motivate in the most difficult moments, and encourage them to leave their comfort zone when necessary. Goleman says a team led by an executive with significant EI exceeds their goals by 20%.[1]

To cope with virtual relations forced by COVID-19, executives must increase their *Digital Empathy*, becoming more receptive, sensitive, and expert listener to calibrate their communication with physically distant collaborators.

---

[1] Goleman D.1998. "What Makes a Leader?" *Harvard Business Review- reprint R0401H*

CHAPTER 6

The Setback

Monday, 10:00 a.m.

"Good morning Andrew, how are you? We have a meeting to review the channel project. Do you want me to find a meeting room or should we meet here at your desk?" Katherine's first review with Andrew is about to start.

"Here is fine, please take a seat. Elisabeth gave me an update and I would like to better understand in which direction you are moving."

Katherine was expecting it: Elisabeth and Andrew continue their direct communication...

She is prepared, however, and ready to handle questions of all kinds. She immediately unlocks her notebook and opens her presentation. She starts with a few points summary of the overall situation, then she continues adding more details in the following slides. She often looks at Andrew to see if he has any feedback to make sure her presentation is clear or if he has any questions.

Andrew does not interrupt her; every now and then he nods, impassive, signaling with his eyes to go on. Katherine doesn't know how to interpret Andrew's unspoken communication. So, she tries to focus on the content. She illustrates all the relevant points and after about 20 minutes she closes with "Andrew, this is how we have set the project up and what we have developed so far. I have more detailed information and data if you would like to go deeper."

Andrew nods, thoughtfully, and for a few long seconds, he says nothing. However, it is not the typical nodding of those who agree. Katherine begins to fidget but she tries to control her emotions.

"A lot of work, Katherine, but honestly you are off track."

Katherine swallows, looking down. Andrew is definitely not tactful: She has to separate his style from the business considerations, avoid being overwhelmed by emotions, and rather try to remain calm and remember what Mary told her yesterday.

"Please tell me more, Andrew. We are still in the initial phases: We can change our direction if it makes more sense."

"The problem is that you are only investigating some aspects and it is quite theoretical. You are not considering its feasibility, or actually how to generate a business impact out of your initiatives. This is not a university dissertation: It is a business project that must be implemented to deliver results. It has to be executable and affordable to be real."

It is not easy to listen to such a harsh and perhaps too hasty judgment, but Katherine makes an effort to listen, resisting the temptation to defend her work. On the contrary, she takes notes on her notepad to convey the impression of being open to change.

"Various things are missing, but most of all you are not considering how our business processes actually work. First of all, our budgeting cycle. Your plan might be fine in theory, but there is no point in thinking about submitting a fund request 2 weeks after budgets are allocated. Similarly, the program review must take place before and not after the fiscal year earning announcement; otherwise, it is completely useless to answer any questions from the investors."

"I get it. Let me take it with the team. I don't think there are any problems in adjusting our deadlines."

"Look, that's just one of the problems. I'll tell you another one: inventory management and the production cycle. They are never mentioned in your project. It looks like you're sprinting, but this is a relay. You have to take the baton and you have to pass it. What are the implications for Manufacturing? And for Procurement?"

"We don't know: It's too early to say."

"Sure, we don't know, but we know they will be important. Production and Procurement will need time to prepare. What worries me is not that you don't know yet, but the fact that you aren't asking the question. In the project you presented to me, I saw a lot of details, but all in one direction only... give me an update next week, now sorry but I have to ask you to go because I am expecting an important phone call."

And so saying, Andrew turns to his PC screen. He has already moved on to the next topic.

Katherine thanks, greets, receives no reply, and starts to go back to her desk. It was tough: not a single positive remark about the work done. Is it possible that Andrew has not seen that listening to the resellers has already revealed that our current strategy is based on at least 3 major, wrong, or obsolete assumptions? She was clear; her presentation was well articulated. Really didn't Andrew see the value of the work already done?

At this point, tea is a must, indeed perhaps a chamomile tea would be better...

Back from this short break, Katherine reads her notes again and she must admit that her boss is brusque, but certainly not stupid and... he's not wrong. Indeed, frankly he is definitely right.

She let herself be fascinated by the first results of their work and lost sight of the so-called "big picture," the overall context. She chose to take a Design Thinking approach, but she lost sight of the feasibility of the project. She leads a multidisciplinary team, but, in fact, she has only a limited business perspective.

It was she who was wrong. Without realizing it, she put on the blinders. She did a great job *in* the project (Andrew didn't say it this way, but that's it, damn it!), but the details made her blind: She focused on the trees, missing the forest. She overlooked the impact, the consequences, and the dependencies with the rest of the organization: the other functions, processes, and teams.

She focused on optimizing a piece, hers, but not necessarily the whole. Now Katherine sees exactly what Andrew meant.

She smiles, thinking about the concept of antifragility: Will she be able to benefit from the conversation with Andrew, seize the opportunity, and propose a more valuable approach?

Maybe, but now her project seems a disaster to her: It's as if Andrew had called her stupid. Now she really has no idea where to start over, how to approach Production and Procurement. Not to mention the budgeting process. Maybe Elisabeth could help her, but she is so hostile. Another internal help could be James, who, coming from Finance, should know the company budgeting process well. Yeah, James... shouldn't he have given you an update 2 days ago? Instead, he was neither seen nor heard...

Deep Dive—Business Acumen

Business acumen is the ability to effectively and efficiently predict, interpret, and manage a business situation weighing both risks and opportunities. It is having a clear, strategic *big picture*, knowing how the company works and anticipating the implications of each decision.

Having business acumen means being *on* the business, namely to focus on the success of the business as a whole and not on the needs of a single function or business unit (which would imply being *in* the business). It means interpreting analytics, listening to the market, prioritizing the benefit of the company to the interest of one part. It means confronting with colleagues to collect inputs and ideas, understanding the value generated by the company along the entire production chain, partners and suppliers included (see Figure 6.1 and Table 6.1 for details).

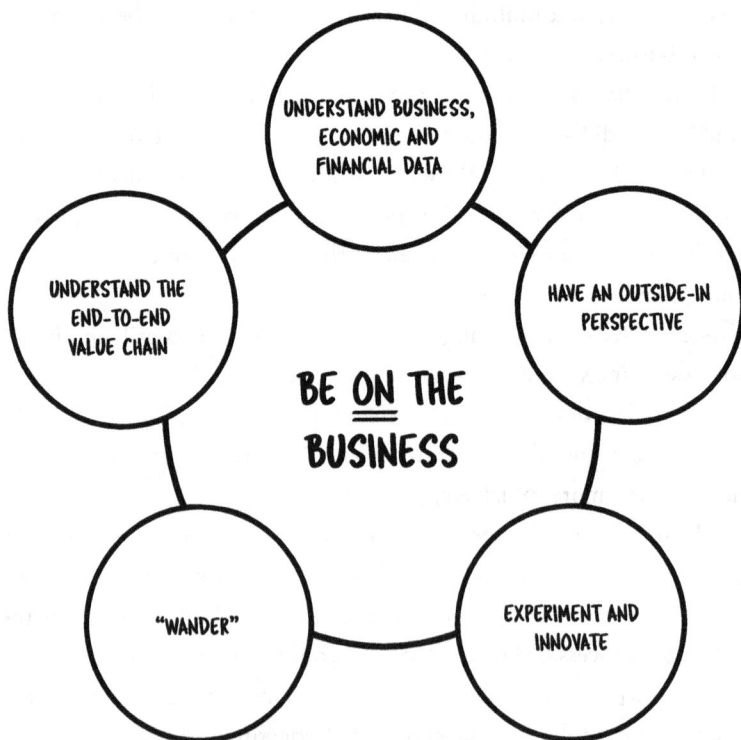

Figure 6.1 Be on the business

Credits: Sebastiano Boni

Having business acumen implies being a sort of chief executive officer (CEO), who prioritizes the need of the entire company to that of a single business unit, guaranteeing the best returns in the short, medium, and long terms.

In the last years, the concept of business acumen has evolved and has been reinterpreted according to contemporary needs. It has moved on from being strongly focused on the existing business model to leveraging business information, knowledge, and experience to empower new approaches aimed at designing future solutions. Therefore, business acumen has become a valid ally, not a brake, on innovation and Design Thinking.

Table 6.1 Key questions about being on the business

What is needed to be on the business?	Key questions
Correctly understand and interpret business, economic, and financial data	• Do you correctly understand business, economic, and financial data? • What is their implication in the short, medium, and long terms? • Do you correctly prioritize the initiatives you sponsor? • What are the impacts of the initiatives you currently sponsor?
Have an outside-in perspective	• Do you listen to the market? • Do your initiatives respond to client needs?
Experiment and innovate	• Are you open to experimentation and innovation or, on the opposite, are you fixed to your company's traditional business model?
Manage by wandering around	• Do you wander, meet, listen to, and provoke feedback from colleagues at all levels? • Do you learn from and leverage ideas and information gathered? • Do you recognize talent?
Understand the end-to-end value chain	• Do you know your company's end-to-end value chain? • Do you recognize the value and the contribution of each function to the company's business? • Do you understand how your company does business and interacts with suppliers and partners? What are their value and contribution?

CHAPTER 7

Reset With a Friend

"Hi Mary, this is Katherine. How are you?"

"I am great, thank you but... you? From your voice, you don't sound really well."

"That's it. I called you to check whether you had some time for me."

"Gladly. Let me look... this afternoon around 3 p.m.?"

"That would be perfect, thanks. See you later."

***

When it is time, Katherine climbs upstairs to the HR Department. Mary smiles at her from behind her desk, PC off, hands on the table. Katherine is amazed at how some top executives manage to give the impression of being always available and ready to listen, while certainly, they have a hectic agenda.

"You are always on time, I was waiting for you. Do you want to continue our conversation on attitude and antifragility?"

"Yes and no. I certainly feel very fragile now, Mary. In fact, I feel lost..."

Quickly Katherine updates her on the project, Andrew's feedback, James' disengagement, and Elisabeth's hostility.

"Ok, one thing at a time. Let's start from the beginning: What is the goal?"

"The goal of the project?"

"Both, the project's and yours."

"Our market channel share is declining rapidly, so the goal is to understand how to review the current strategy and reverse the trend."

"And how will you be able to say that the trend has reversed?"

It sounds like a trivial question, but it isn't. Katherine reflects for a moment, then: "Obviously we measure the sales we make through the channel. I believe that as a first step we want to stop the decline, it would be the first positive sign. Then the decline must shift to growth."

"Can you be more specific?"

"Yes sure. I don't want to throw a random number, let me work with the team on this. I believe that growth can be any number higher than the average market growth. It would be a sign that we are gaining share."

"And by when have you set out to reach these thresholds of lower decline, growth, and above average growth?"

The question is so obvious that Katherine wonders how she didn't think about it herself: "I don't know. I was not told and I didn't think to clarify it. You're absolutely right. For now, let's say we want to stop the decrease within 6 months, put a positive sign in front of our numbers within 12, and be above the market average within 18. But I will work on it."

"Well, for now, let's work with these assumptions you just said. If you reach these goals, what is the outcome for the company?"

"Again, I don't know, Mary, but once more you're right. The impact would be enormous: first on the turnover. Then, given our cost structure, the benefit would be even higher on margins and this would mean more spending capacity in Research and Development and therefore an increase in our brand reputation."

"Can you quantify these impacts?"

"Sure, I have to work on it, but it shouldn't be too difficult. In case I have any problems, I can ask the CFO for support."

"May I tell you my point of view?"

"I'm here for this..."

"Speak to the CFO anyway. Even if you come up with perfect calculations, dealing with someone outside the team always adds perspective and credibility. If you present some turnover and margin numbers that you have previously discussed with the CFO and got his stamp, nobody will argue or say that you are wrong."

Katherine nods and Mary continues: "Now, let's keep going with our reasoning: Even without accurate numbers, and considering only a bulk estimate, how important are these results for you, personally?"

"Very important." Katherine responds with no hesitation, then she reflects and adds, lowering her voice: "For the company, from what I see, it is fundamental. We are not doing as well as it looks. The situation is more serious than they say, but perhaps you, given your role, are already aware of it."

"Yes, it is as you say. Tell me about yourself: How important are the results for Kathy?"

"Same, very important. It is my first real big project, in total autonomy. I am facing enormous challenges, but I know that this is the best way to learn. From 1 to 10: 10!"

"Ok... you've already told me about the situation before: As you said, it's challenging but clear. What options do you see moving forward?"

"I believe that it makes sense to let Mark and Maurice continue the task they started because it is giving good results, anyway. I just have to reframe it in a broader context."

"So, what are you proposing?"

"I have to take care of the objectives myself, but I can get James to help me. He comes from Finance: He can be of great help in validating my assumptions and he can help me prepare for the meeting with the CFO."

"And then?"

"I need to address the shortcomings highlighted by Andrew. I could ask Elisabeth for them. It suits her skills: She comes from Operations, and she has been working with Production and Procurement before."

"What else? Is there anyone else who could be involved? Who will be the main recipient of your work?"

"Sales obviously, and in particular those working on channel. How would you engage them, Mary?"

"I'd like to hear your opinion first."

Another question that is only apparently simple...

"I'd say the same way you started with me earlier: Share our goal and timing and ask them if they believe they're relevant."

"OK... then will you ask them for something concrete? Can they help you in any way?"

"Sure. Now a new world is opening up to me, Mary: I absolutely have to ask them to validate our assumptions. First, I need to check whether the numbers I discuss with the CFO are feasible from their point of view: The implementation of the project will actually pass through them because they are our Channel Account Managers and they negotiate priorities with our partners."

"OK... Now, how do you plan to put these activities in priority order?"

Another moment of silence, Katherine needs to figure it out: "Clarifying the objectives is the first thing: Without those, I cannot effectively engage the stakeholders and ask for a contribution. It is even more difficult to motivate the team if the objectives are not clear."

"Ok... What about considering even 1 or 2 simple actions, which allow building positive energy and visibility around the project?"

"A quick win: That's a great point! I have an idea about it, I'm working on it... Mary: I don't know how to thank you, you have been fantastic, as usual. You opened my eyes and helped me to see the way forward."

As they stand up to say goodbye, Mary adds: "It's always a pleasure, Kathy. However, be aware that you found the solution yourself: I only asked you a few questions. By the way, how about meeting again in 2 weeks so we can review the progress?"

Thinking back, that's exactly what happened. Mary was just asking questions and while doing so, she was focused and relaxed, while Katherine was literally sweating to find intelligent answers to the goads she was receiving. The result, however, has been amazing.

Right tomorrow there is a new team meeting. Katherine feels ready, more aware, and fully motivated.

Deep Dive—GROW Model

Certainly, one of the best-known coaching models, the GROW model can help all the leaders in their daily conversations with their collaborators. The model enables a structured, goal-oriented conversation, aimed at developing a creative and *generative thinking* and achieving results. GROW is the acronym for:

- G—Goal
- R—Reality
- O—Options
- W—Will

Once the subject (Topic) and the objective of the conversation (Goal) have been set and agreed upon, it is important to analyze the current situation (Reality) and all the possible alternatives (Options) to achieve the desired result, identifying the action plan (Will) with the timeline, resources, and actions to ensure results. See Figure 7.1.

Let's analyze the GROW process.

- *Goal:* Once the topic of the conversation has been clarified, it is important to first define and agree on the goal which must be SMART, namely:
  - S—Specific (instead of generic)
  - M—Measurable (in terms of results)
  - A—Achievable
  - R—Realistic
  - T—Timeframed (temporally identified)

  If the topic is complex, it will be necessary to clarify both the macro-objective (e.g., definition of the commercial strategy to increase sales by 20% in this fiscal year) and the specific objective for the conversation of the day (e.g., definition of the commercial strategy to increase sales by 20% in this fiscal year for product X). Starting the conversation from the goal might seem unintuitive to some people, but it allows you to project yourself into the future and not get lost in discussions about past mistakes or situations which could be dysfunctional and time consuming to achieve the preset goal.

It is always advisable to translate the goal into the *outcome* (e.g., 3 strategic directions to increase sales of product *X* by 20% in this fiscal year) and verify its *importance* for the counterparts, checking and stimulating their motivation. (From 1 to 10 how much important is it for you to make 20% more sales than last year?)

- *Reality*: Some information on current or past situations may be key to inform strategies and achieve the desired result. The advice is to limit this type of information exclusively to the relevant details needed to guide the following step.

- *Options*: This is certainly the most creative phase, in which provoking new ideas is essential to identify the best option to achieve the goal. As in Design Thinking, initially quantity is more important than quality.

The following questions are all useful to boost creativity and add alternatives:

  o What do you propose?
  o In the absence of constraints, what would you do?
  o What else?
  o Looking at this situation from outside, what advice would you give a friend in your situation?
  o Take 3 people you respect professionally, how would they act in this situation? Could there be further options to consider?

For example, if the objective is to define 3 strategic directions, at this stage it is good to create a list that is at least 2 or 3 times longer (in the example, 6 to 9 options).

What if the coachee has no ideas? Or ask the executive for help? In this case, the leader can provoke creative thinking, suggesting multiple options (at least 2 or 3) without sharing any personal preference and avoiding influencing the collaborator to choose the one that the executive favors.

Once the list of alternatives has been established, the collaborator must narrow it down and select the best option based on the expected benefits, its feasibility, and accountability, which must be with the coachee.

The analysis and choice of the best option is the employee's responsibility, but the leader can contribute in 2 ways:

  o *Observation and intuition*: The leader can share a perception or an intuition that comes from the careful observation of the collaborator (e.g., While you were speaking, I noticed that your tone changed when you mentioned option 1. Can you help me to better understand your instinctive reaction?).

  o Brainstorming: The leader can contribute to the brainstorming with their own reflections and perspectives.

- *Will*: The last phase is action planning. It is necessary to define the necessary actions to implement the option chosen in the previous phase and specify the resources, timeline, and possibly the people who need to be involved for contributions or approvals. The *Will* is the phase in which the real action plan is drawn.

In order for the model to work, there are a few tricks to apply:

- *Listening*: Listening must be attentive, free, and open.

  o Attentive: To allow the executive to grasp the words and all the additional signals coming from the nonverbal and para-verbal communication (tones and rhythms of the voice) of the collaborator. The executive must, therefore, listen with big eyes, open heart, and an emotional belly!

  o Free: To allow the executive to follow the logical flow of the collaborator without thinking about what to say next.

  o Open: To avoid the influence of prejudice, assumptions, beliefs.

  For this to happen, the executives will have to devote themselves completely to their collaborators, avoiding interruptions or interferences such as e-mails, phone calls, messages that, by distracting them, defocus from the main object of listening. The employees will recognize all this attention, feel like the priority, and reward their manager with a higher engagement.

- *Accountability*: Coaching is based on the individual's responsibility. The action plan, therefore, must include tasks that the collaborator can control. If there are activities that need to be carried out by others, the collaborator will act as *project manager* and ensure the execution of others' tasks in the preestablished ways and timeline.

- *Questions*: The GROW model and coaching recognize the importance of questions to stimulate the cognitive process. Each of us is, in fact, more at ease with thoughts, answers, and solutions developed autonomously compared to those forced by others. Hence, the importance of provoking personal reflection through questions. To work, questions must be:
  - ○ Open: They should not imply a yes/no answer, but allow the employees to think through and generate their own answers (e.g., "What is the best customer target to increase sales by 20% year over year?" is very different from saying "To increase sales by 20%, would you only target large customers?").
  - ○ Powerful and transformative: They must act like reagents developing a process of transformation, increasing awareness in the employee, enlightening the reality with new perspectives, pushing to explore, and get out of the comfort zone.

However, the GROW approach produces the best results if applied in a safe, judgment-free environment built on preexisting trust between the executive and the collaborator.

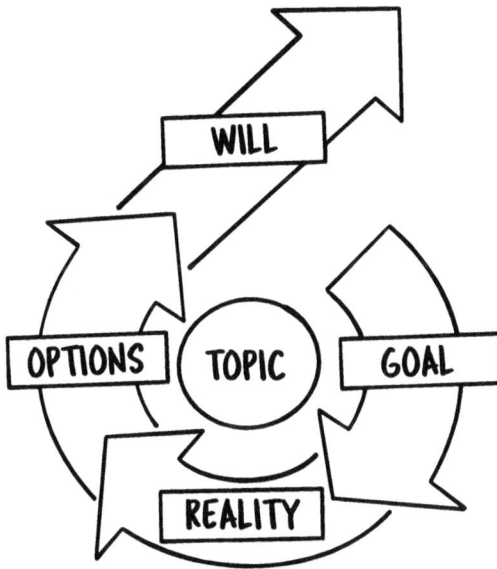

Figure 7.1 GROW *model*

Credits: Sebastiano Boni

CHAPTER 8

Finally

Tuesday.

The team meeting went very well. The greater clarity about the goals gave everyone a sense of direction.

Everyone in the team is now at work leveraging their strengths. On paper, it is not different than before: Since the beginning Katherine had been careful to assign tasks that were as close as possible to individual experiences, but now something has clicked for each one, a motivation that wasn't there before.

Even Elisabeth agreed with the stated goals and she started working in teamwork with the others. Finally, she feels that her seniority is recognized and she is conscious that she can move autonomously in the area where she can add the highest value.

Mark and Maurice already had high motivation before, but now their influence is more effective. Nobody is anymore questioning the importance of listening to the market, partners, and customers. Their contribution has become more precise and cutting edge because they use the project objectives to focus their research work.

And now that the objectives are clearer and the climate is collaborative, Elisabeth has proved to be a precious and respected critic. Maurice shared that it was thanks to one of her insights that Mark and he went to investigate an aspect previously neglected. And this sparked a discovery that seems to be the key to redesigning the channel incentive system.

James feels part of the group. He is more self-confident; he feels that there is no prejudgment about his ideas, but only the desire for him to contribute to the success of the project.

Katherine keeps Andrew regularly informed and he seems to like the direction the project is now taking. Katherine's days are more productive and this reflects on her mood.

Even at home. After dinner, after clearing the table, Luke rushes to his room to play some video games. Thomas and Katherine are left alone: "How did it go today? From your face, I would say that last week's problems are being sorted out?"

"I would say so, eventually. I'm happy with how things are going at work. It is as if the engine has finally started up and it is now running at full speed."

"Are you talking about your team?"

"Yes, but not only that. The same is true for how we interlock with the other functions and the other business processes. The interesting thing is that it looks like we have created a virtuous circle. I wasn't expecting it, even if, with hindsight, it is quite logical."

"What is that?"

"The executives talk to each other. The more they have the opportunity to see the project and give their opinion, the more likely they are to talk about it with a colleague or with their team and this generates further connections and points of view. Managers and teams that I did not even know existed are now calling me to find out more and offer collaboration."

"In mechanics, it's called momentum. It is the mass of an object multiplied by its speed," smiles Thomas who is a manager in a mechanical company.

"Ah, I thought it was called luck..."

"Why luck?"

"Because I still don't understand what I did, or if something happened independently of me that triggered this virtuous circle."

"The credit is all yours and you should take it, Katherine. Based on what you told me last night, you 'simply' created the conditions that are most favorable for collaboration. And it's not that simple."

"But... what have I done?" laughs Katherine.

"You have done 2 things that may seem contradictory, but they are not: You have created a team, which moves together toward one goal, with consistent and shared metrics, the same sense of urgency. And at the same time, everyone in the team has their own space, which fits with their own way of being and working, which is different for each of us."

"Are you saying that we are all in the same boat, but one is at the helm, one is at the sails, one is maneuvering the anchor, and so on?"

"More or less, but with a specific rationale. Being all in the same boat, of which everyone knows the direction is fundamental. But you also put at the helm those who best know the sea currents, at the sails those who have a sixth sense for the winds... so everyone contributes to the best of their abilities because they are in the right role, they enjoy it, they feel that their contribution is important and appreciated. Everyone, being the expert in a given area, knows that they have the right degree of autonomy, or confidence if you prefer, in tensioning the rigging or whatever else they have to do."

"Yes, there is a lot of mutual respect and a lot of trust in the team now."

"You created it. It is the leader's job and you did it very well, even if you may not even have noticed it... Shall I make you some limoncello to celebrate?"

"Go for the limoncello." Katherine smiles and happily awaits the prize for her first, unexpected success.

Deep Dive—Collaboration and Teamwork

Now more than ever, teams are called upon to collaborate. Now more than ever, the limitation of independence, the uncertainty for the future, the logistical and cultural distance create fear, difficulty, disengagement. Now more than ever, executives play an important role in building a collaborative environment and transferring a functional way of working together.

Neuroscience and sociological studies show that our brains respond to the ancestral threat–reward mechanism. Every human being, rationally or irrationally, tends to shy away from everything that interprets as a threat and work to maximize the rewards. There are 5 levers (triggers) that can be activated positively, and be interpreted as a reward, or negatively, and be perceived as a threat.

The 5 levers, known under the acronym SCARF, are:

- *Status*: Is the relative importance to others, is the seniority. The exclusion from a project, the lack of responsibility, the assignment of trivial tasks misaligned with personal experience are interpreted by our brain as a threat to our state and seniority. On the contrary, positive feedback and, above all, public recognitions are associated with awards.
- *Certainty*: Is the ability to predict the future. In the presence of inconsistency, lack of clarity on the arguments which justify a request, or uncertainty about the executive's expectations, the brain focuses on the search for truth, wasting energy and resources. On the contrary, reassuring collaborators—clarifying expectations, anticipating meeting objectives, breaking project objectives into sub-objectives—reassures and allows individuals to focus on their work.
- *Autonomy*: Is the perception of being able to control ourselves and our actions, having the freedom of choice. Being responsible for and able to make decisions on a project, for example, increase involvement and engagement. Receiving detailed instructions on how to operate (e.g., here's what you need to do...) limits problem solving, creativity, and learning and generates frustration.

- *Relatedness*: Is an affiliation. It is feeling part of a group and therefore safe in the presence of others (self-confidence). Being by collaborators' side, limiting hierarchical distance, and supporting collaboration within the team (instead of competitiveness) create a safe environment, in which to freely propose opinions and ideas.
- *Fairness*: Is honesty, which manifests in impartiality, in the absence of preferences and judgment, in openness and inclusion. The executive must be impartial toward all team members. The concept of fairness is also linked to that of trust.

The executive can, however, operate the 5 SCARF in either a functional or a dysfunctional way:

- The *functional* way will create an environment based on trust and fairness, open to constructive confrontation and diversity of opinions (see Figure 8.1). It will reward commitment and responsibility; learning will be collective; and results will be achieved as a consequence of effective teamwork, rewarded as

Figure 8.1 SCARF-based collaboration

Credits: Sebastiano Boni

part of continuous growth. Neurologically, behaviors that can be interpreted as rewards trigger the production of oxytocin and dopamine with a scientifically proven improvement in creativity, proactivity, problem solving, productivity, motivation, and happiness. Leveraging SCARF functionally will allow guaranteeing effective and sustainable teamwork over time.

- The *dysfunctional way* manifests, for example, in microman-agement or demotion. It may be a habit so ingrained in the leader that it is not even rationalized. The dysfunctional activation of one or more SCARF raises the level of cortisol and generates stress, frustration, disengagement. For example, if executives want to maintain responsibility for every activity, even if operational, their collaborators will not feel motivated to give their best because, in any case, they are not responsible for results.

Increasing mindfulness in their actions, paying attention to reactions, and asking and listening to collaborators allow executives to correct their behavior and promote a way to work based on fairness, sense of belonging, accountability, safety, and acknowledgment of the success achieved by the team.

CHAPTER 9

Presentation to the Board

Friday, 11:30 a.m.

It is finally Friday. It has been a long week, but certainly a productive one. The road finally seems downhill toward the finish line.

"Bi-beep," the internal chat system lights up in the corner of Katherine's screen. She is the CEO's chief of staff: "Hello Katherine, can you type?"

"Yes, sure."

"Next Thursday there is a board meeting. They would like you to present the project you are driving. Are you okay at 15:00?"

Conflicting emotions run through Katherine's mind: amazement, pride, panic, happiness... After all, the question is probably rhetorical, so she hurries to answer: "Sure, 15:00 is no problem, thanks."

Only after answering, it occurs to her that she could have asked a few more questions, like: What are the expectations? How long should the presentation be? Any particular points or questions that the board wants to address? She will send an e-mail asking for more details or she will turn to Andrew, Alessandra, or Mary as they are all members of the board.

Thursday is close: She only has 3 full working days to prepare. Even adding the weekend, time is still short. So, Katherine decides to inform the team immediately and get everyone to help.

She calls for a meeting in half an hour. They are all there and from their faces, it is apparent that they are wondering the reason for the meeting. It is quite unusual for Katherine on such short notice.

When Katherine explains the reason, to her great surprise, they all look at each other and spontaneously start a round of applause. Everyone congratulates her on the opportunity that will give great visibility to everyone's work and they ask her how she intends to prepare the presentation.

"I think we will have to line up everything we have produced so far and present it following a logical thread."

"Katherine, in the past Andrew was asking me to help him when he had to present to the board. His mantra was: 'less is more.'" It is Elisabeth who takes the floor. Finally, without any pedantic or superior tone.

"It is good advice," Mark reinforces, "Present the overall situation and get quickly to the 2 key points where we want approval and support. All the rest are details that may sound irrelevant at that level, raise unnecessary questions, and possibly start defocusing discussions. The more you load the presentation, the higher the risk of running out of time, before reaching a validation on the key points."

"It's the same thing Andrew always said." Elisabeth adds: "They are all smart and well-prepared people. They already know the situation, they have probably talked about it at the board level at other times and many of them have certainly already gone through similar issues at other times, in other boards, in other companies." Then she adds: "An easy way is to organize your presentation in 3 logical steps:

- First present the situation, grounding it on facts and data. Use only information that we can back up with confidence, nothing that can generate arguing or doubts on our credibility. And let's carefully select the numbers we present, they are instrumental in paving the way for the next step.
- Then introduce the problem, or the circumstances that have occurred, what has worsened the situation, reducing our share and margins.
- Finally, the last step: Reveal the solution, which is our recommendation to get out of it."

Katherine listens with great attention: She is also happy that Elisabeth is trying to help. Jokingly she says: "It looks like a tale...!"

"It is!" James intervenes. "It is the typical structure of classical mythology. Movies also often follow a similar structure. Billy Wilder, the famous movie director, suggested a 3-acts model: The first act introduces the hero, the existing relationships with the other characters, and their aspirations. In the second act, the hero faces some obstacles or impediments that keep them away from achieving their desire. In the third and final act, the hero finds a solution. Most of the movies follow this pattern."

James has polarized everyone's attention so he continues: "If you think about it, obstacles create emotions in the public and that's why they are there. The more you want to emotionally involve the audience, the more the authors complicate the situation with problems, unexpected events, etc. A story can be easily remembered and shared, emotions strike, and engage. Those who decide, our board members, must be 'involved' emotionally, not just rationally."

"Where does all this sudden passion come from?" Maurice asks jokingly, "Don't get me wrong: I totally agree with what you're saying."

James reflects for a moment before replying; he is a bit embarrassed. The whole team is watching him: "Well ... as a hobby I am a theater director. I run a small semiprofessional company."

"Wow! A second life." It was Mark who spoke; everyone laughs. Maurice gives a pat on the shoulder to James who, wholeheartedly, continues: "The other thing that theater teaches us is that everything is performance. What you say is of course very important, but how you say it is even more important. Your tone of voice and your gestures must convey confidence."

"Yeah, it's true: I read an article that talked about the 7-38-55 rule." Mark speaks again.

"Which is?" asks Katherine.

"Research says that only 7% of communication goes through speech, 38% through tone of voice, and 55%, by far the largest percentage, through body language."

"Perfect: You convinced me. Let's do this then: Elisabeth, James, can you start developing the story? Mark and Maurice, you will be the 'judges.' Come on, let's start right away... let's write down the basic ideas, then on Monday we take stock and start putting the pieces together. How does it sound to everyone?"

Deep Dive—Foundation of Effective Communication

Each of us communicates. But doing it effectively is a skill of a few. The effectiveness of the communication is measured according to the result we get by communicating: Has our interlocutors received the message we wanted to convey? Did it spark their interest? Did it cause a change: an action, a purchase, or an opinion?

Then, what are the best practices for effective communication? Regardless of the type of communication, the main objective will be to *put our interlocutor at the center, building a personalized, structured, and incisive message that resonates and generates a reaction.* To do this it is necessary to:

- *Define the goal and the desired result*: Communication always determines a change (of perspective, knowledge, action, and so on). It is necessary to clarify our goal in advance (inform, discuss, motivate, encourage action, ...) and the result we want to achieve to determine the direction of our communication.
- *Know the interlocutor/audience*: In front of us we have people with specific needs, habits, beliefs, tastes, and levels of knowledge. They are influenced by their system of values, aspirations, and emotions and by that of family members, peers, influencers, role models, and so on. Therefore, to be effective in our communication, we will have to:
  - Research our interlocutor or audience's needs, habits, beliefs, preferences.
  - "Put us in their shoes" and foresee:
    - What they may want—Is their need aligned with our goal and the result we want to achieve?
    - How they can react to our message—What objections should we expect? How can we handle them?

  Finally, we will have to understand what they already know about the topic and select what information to insert or omit in our communication, building an ad hoc message for our interlocutor and avoiding being repetitive or generic.
- Identify *#1 big idea*: This is the core of our communication. It is the main message that we want to convey and influence

our counterpart. It is the idea around which we build the communication and the call to action. And... "Less is more"—a single idea, supported and correctly structured, is better than a multitude of thoughts that are difficult to remember.

- Structuring the story (*storytelling*): With the emergence of Design Thinking and Human Centricity, storytelling has been confirmed as the most effective means of communication. A story, in fact, can be easily understood, remembered, and shared. It brings concreteness to an abstract and/or theoretical message. As in movies, the story has a protagonist around whom the plot revolves, so an effective storytelling has a character at the core and a big idea around which the narration is articulated. The latter must hook, involve, surprise, and finally reassure the interlocutor. To be effective, the structure of the story will have to follow a precise and predefined flow, often detailed operationally in a storyboard. Typically, the story features:
  - The main and, possibly, the secondary characters
  - The current situation (reality)
  - The desired situation
  - The gap between the current and the desired state
  - The action plan to implement the desired state

  The interlocutor's engagement increases adding humor, questions, polls to the story

- Consider the main *channel of the interlocutor's information assimilation*: The communication must consider the coexistence of verbal and visual, logical and emotional components in different percentages depending on the interlocutor. The learning channels are:
  - *Visual*: Visual people absorb and share information through images, graphics, and concepts. They prefer short, fast, and structured communication (bullet point), complemented by images, graphics, and numbers. Without the visual component, they get bored and lose attention.
  - *Auditory*: Auditory people prefer words (written or heard), request and express themselves with excellent linguistic correctness, and consider the visual part as optional.

○ *Kinesthetic*: Kinesthetic people prefer sensations and emotions to logical communication. Without an emotional, tactile, tasting, olfactory experience they will not be able to fully understand the message. Inspirational and value messages, shared experiences, and demos are essential for this target.

Getting the communication channel wrong has a direct impact on communication effectiveness. For example, take communication between a visual and an auditory. The visual will probably see the auditory as too wordy, inefficient, and ineffective. On the contrary, the auditory will consider the visual quick, hasty, sometimes almost rude.

If we face an audience, it is advisable to adopt a comprehensive, integrated style that covers all the communication channels. This guarantees to be effective with all.

• Working on *non-verbal and para-verbal communication*— More than 90% of communication is made up of posture, facial gestures, eye contact (non-verbal), tone, pauses, and rhythm of the voice (para-verbal communication). Knowing how to manage the non-verbal and the para-verbal contributes to the effectiveness of our communication and the assimilation of information. The general rule is to emphasize the most relevant words or ideas by turning up the volume/tone of the voice and slowing down the pace. The breaks, on the other hand, are excellent allies to create space for reflection. Let us remember, however, that para-verbal communication is always influenced by our interlocutors: If they speak fast, our average pace must be fast; if it is slow, we will have to calibrate and pace their mode.

Figure 9.1 Effective communication

Credits: Sebastiano Boni

CHAPTER 10

How Did It Go?

Thursday afternoon, 3:30 p.m.

At the end of her presentation, Katherine leaves the boardroom without understanding how it went...

In the aisle, she stops at an empty desk and tries to recap for herself...

She arrived early, to be sure: approximately 15 minutes before her presentation was scheduled. They let her in a bit late. But she thought this is probably normal for this type of meeting.

At the first glance, she received an excellent impression from the Board of Directors. There were about 20 people in the room, more than strictly the board members who—she checked on the company website—are only a dozen. She knew about half of the participants, those who work in the company and who, although not necessarily members of the Board of Directors, are often invited to attend. However, she had never seen the external members before: university professors, lawyers, and executives from other companies.

As Elisabeth had foreseen, it was immediately clear that everyone was already quite knowledgeable about the channel issues.

It seemed to her that she had set out all the points which she had prepared, with logic, and supporting each assertion with data and facts.

She was a little uncomfortable in unraveling the narrative; she felt like those who know a good tale but are not good at telling it. She is convinced that James' suggestions are absolutely valid, but she was a bit in awe of all those blue jackets, ties, and gray suits and so she tried to rush too quickly to the point.

Katherine's thoughts are interrupted by Andrew's voice, who has left the room even though the meeting is not over: "Hi Katherine."

"Yes, tell me everything." Katherine hopes for a positive comment...

"Can I give you a feedback?"

Ouch, that doesn't bode well!

"Sure, please!"

"You sounded a bit vague in the meeting."

"Why do you say so? I presented data, analysis, as well as our interpretation."

"Yes, but it was all quite generic. It wasn't clear if you had a proposal."

"What sounded generic to you?" while she reminds herself not to become defensive.

"Frankly everything... I'm sure that if I asked the participants what your recommendation is or which action you advised us to take, they wouldn't be able to answer. Now I have to go. I just wanted to give you a quick feedback, we'll talk about it later. Bye."

"Ok, thanks... good continuation."

He knows exactly how to demotivate someone, thinks Katherine after Andrew has returned to the meeting, leaving her with generic and certainly not very constructive criticisms.

She doesn't want to make the same mistake and discourage the team, now that they have started to work well together. Katherine writes a high-level and undetailed message to the team; she simply thanks everyone for their help, says that the presentation went well and that she will know more in the next few days after hearing some opinions.

Then she writes a WhatsApp to Alessandra, asking her if she has a few minutes for her at the end of the board meeting.

It is Alessandra herself who passes by Katherine shortly after. Right thumb up, she starts smiling at Katherine from the end of the corridor: "Congratulations on your first presentation to the board. After you left, the CEO said it's executives like you who give him confidence in the company's future."

"Really? So, it wasn't a complete disaster?"

"Disaster? Far from it! You have given a complete and well-documented picture of the situation. As you may have noticed, all the participants were aware of the data, but it was very useful to see them summarized in a single overall picture. The point where you were most effective was when you compared our data with those from market research and highlighted the differences with quoted comments from channel partners. Do you know what I am referring to? It was one of the first slides..."

"Yes, I understand. We sweated a lot to put it all together."

"Well, it worked great."

"But overall, I'm not sure if I have brought home the result..."

"What result did you set for yourself?"

"Convince the board that the market has changed radically in recent years and we must adapt to make up for lost ground?"

"Is it a question or a statement?"

"A statement," smiles Katherine.

"Is there a point in your presentation where you could have been more assertive or clearer to achieve this goal?"

"Looking back, I think I have only outlined possible scenarios, without taking a clear position."

"Look, in my opinion, the point where you could have been more decisive was when the CEO asked you what your recommendation was out of the 3 scenarios you presented. I, as I think everyone, understood that you strongly leaned toward the 'B' scenario. But in front of the specific question, you have not taken a position."

"Yes, it's true. 'B' is the best scenario, but because of the way the question was formulated, I had the impression that the CEO was for the 'A' scenario and so I thought I'd take a more... let's say cautious position?"

"I don't know if the CEO had a scenario in mind, but I think he was genuinely interested in your expert opinion. You are the one who has analyzed the problem deeper than anyone else, you have been called to give your opinion in addition to the results of the analysis."

"So, a disaster as Andrew made me understand?"

"Far from it! Expect to be summoned again soon. Don't worry about how Andrew expresses himself; sometimes he is too abrupt, but he was happy too and he said so. At the end of the meeting, during the final round table of comments, he said that we have put the right leader on the channel problem."

"Really? So why does he criticize me every time?!"

"Do not worry. He is like that, but he is not a fool: He knows how to recognize the value. And, if you have been wrong in something, this will help you learn. We all make mistakes: the important thing is to learn to overcome them and do better next time. Just think that, at my first presentation to the board, I did not even show up..."

"How is that possible?"

"I should have presented after lunch. I was so focused on rehearsing that I decided to turn off e-mail to avoid any distraction. However, because of some issues, they decided to change the agenda and anticipate my speech late in the morning. Bottom line, when I showed up, perfectly on time, but on the old schedule, they sent me back."

"What a story, but then you made a career anyway."

"In fact, so there is hope for you too," closes Alessandra, laughing and winking at Catherine.

Alessandra's feedback has finally given back courage to Katherine. Before going home, she wants to set up the work for the next few days: The board asked to test the scenarios in the field and get some feedback, to validate or correct the assumptions that emerged.

"Doing is the best way to learn," so said the CEO. Better take note and take action!

Deep Dive—Feedback

Key for the team's growth, feedback is a practice to be handled with care. Neuroscience has shown that the question "Can I share my feedback?" generates a defensive reaction in the interlocutor—the spontaneous reaction of the amygdala and the secretion of cortisol (stress hormone). Therefore, it is convenient for the executive to follow some simple rules and leverage on the feedback as an enabler of continuous growth:

- *Trust*: This is the a priori condition that allows us to share, accept, and perceive feedback as a constructive practice and a useful input to collaborate and grow together.
- *Structure*: The best feedback follows a precise structure (see Figure 10.1). Executives have to:
  1. Start with an *appreciative analysis* (what went well and needs to be replicated), specifying *why* and *how* the collaborator did a good job. Then, executives have to analyze concrete facts and extract strengths to reinforce the collaborator's identity and finally identify progress and lesson learnt to build their growth mindset.
  2. Ask the collaborator to identify *areas for possible improvement* (what could have been done better) and the impact of the decisions made or behaviors held.
  3. Ask the collaborator to identify the *desired outcomes* and discuss them together.
  4. Ask the collaborator to identify the *actions or behavioral changes needed* to achieve the desired outcomes.
  5. Ask the interlocutor to *summarize the conversation*.
- *Examples, evidence, and facts*: Feedback must be specific and based on evidence and facts. It shouldn't be abstract or generalize a single behavior. This objectifies the conversation, avoiding abstract discussions, possible arguments, and waste of time.
- *Transformative language*: Language is important to create a climate of growth. The best feedback leverages a language that recalls and inspires transformation (e.g., develop, create, build), without being either judgmental (e.g., you were *wrong*) or directive (e.g., you *must not*, you *cannot*).

- *Timing*: It is important to share our feedback as soon as possible and make the feedback practice part of the team culture. This will avoid stress and fear associated with the formal, yearly performance evaluation and will help boost people's development.
- *Reciprocity of feedback* (executive–collaborator; collaborator–executive): Neuroscience confirms that even just the perception of openness and the possibility to share bottom-up feedback (from the collaborator to the executive) feeds the need for honesty and equality, limits the collaborator's fear of judgment, and contributes to creating a safe environment for further top-down feedback.

The impact of poor feedback is much stronger than the one associated with powerful feedback. So, let's learn how to use this powerful practice to the best to maximize its benefit and avoid negative impacts.

Figure 10.1 Feedback and appreciative analysis

Credits: Sebastiano Boni

CHAPTER 11

First Rollout

Friday.

Sleeping on it always lets you see everything more clearly.

Katherine fully embraced Alessandra's feedback on how the presentation went: She could have been more assertive, more self-confident, but all in all, it didn't go badly. Rereading her notes, it is apparent that the board gave both priorities and several guidelines on how to move forward.

She decides that she will share the feedback with the team also because she wants to continue using their support and insights for the next presentation, but now: all the focus on execution!

When she spoke to the CSO, Hans Mayer, he insisted on the importance of organizing execution in clear workflows, with clear objectives and clear responsibilities. Yesterday, on the sidelines of her presentation, he had renewed his invitation and promised to put her in contact with a person from his team to help her.

While having breakfast, Katherine opens the e-mail and finds an e-mail from Hans to Kamila, to which Kamila has already replied, proposing a video call for mid-morning.

Kamila is Polish, speaks excellent English, with a typical accent. She is young and immediately stands out for her practical sense.

"Katherine, I can help you create a PMO."

"One thing at a time, Kamila. What is a PMO?"

"PMO stands for Project Management Office. But it is not necessarily a real office. It can also be done by one person, depending on the complexity. The PMO is a back-office function that provides operational and methodological support for the management and coordination of one or more projects."

"Practically?"

"First of all, it defines, together with you, how each project should be organized, which metrics you want to use to track their progress, and how often you want to receive a progress update."

"This would actually be very useful."

"It is also responsible for facilitating communication and synchronization between subprojects. So, if a project develops something that can be useful to another project, the PMO is activated to create the link."

"So PMO is made up of geniuses who know everything?"

"Well, thanks... but no, they're not people who know everything; for that we already have managers like you, Katherine."

Kamila is really smart, with a good sense of humor, and she is not afraid of confronting those who are more senior than her.

"The person in charge of the PMO must be flexible, fast, and above all must not be shy in asking questions and reminding the deadlines."

"Well, my team is small and they are all busy with the various streams of the project. Could you give me a hand and let's set it up together?"

"Yes, of course, that's exactly what Hans asked me. To get started, I would like to check how strong our PMO is."

"What do you mean?"

"It's my personal theory. Independently of the business issue that the project is addressing and the quality of the work that is being developed, 4 key factors determine the success of the PMO and they are sponsorship, simplicity, communication, and cadence.

Or at least I call them this way."

Kamila sees that Katherine is taking notes, so she stops for a moment to let her write, then she explains:

"The sponsors are the ones who care about the project and they make sure that the people we need will pay attention to our requests."

"I guess a good sponsor is proactive in showing the importance of it."

"It is very important. Proactivity and authenticity! The second key factor is simplicity. This is essential in explaining to people what we expect from them. As Einstein said: 'If you can't explain it in simple terms, you don't understand it well enough. So, simplicity is also needed for my third point, which is communication.'"

"Internal communication or external to Apold?"

"Especially internal. Like all transformation processes, we will have to explain over and over again why, how, and what we are doing, at all levels. And we must also always be open to listening."

"And the fourth factor did you say is cadence?"

"Yes, cadence. We have to be regular and predictable like the swing of a pendulum, both toward the subproject leaders and toward the sponsors."

"Give me an example, please."

"For example, we may want to ask the leaders of each subproject to give us an update every week, on Fridays, by noon. With the stakeholders, vice versa, we may want to create the expectation of a monthly e-mail update, and then obviously we need to do it. A regular cadence precisely."

"I get it. In fact, these key factors seem closely related to each other. Without simplicity, it is difficult to win over sponsors and it is difficult to communicate clearly. Sponsors need results, so they will appreciate the cadence, which will be especially visible in the way we communicate."

"Exactly. Sponsor side we are in good shape."

"You mean the CEO?"

"Maybe, but it's hard to expect operational involvement from the CEO. I was thinking of Hans. This project is essential for sales and Hans is an excellent sponsor: He likes to help projects that transform the company and make us more modern and more competitive."

After a short pause, Kamila continues: "Do you want me to prepare a proposal for how we could organize the PMO for this project and then you and I will review it together? What about Monday afternoon?"

"Thank you very much, Kamila! It would be great. You are fast! In a short time, we have covered a lot of work."

Deep Dive—Execution

How often have you met colleagues, excellent strategists, or skilled speakers who were *not* execution-oriented? How often have you participated in never-ending meetings, joined long-lasting projects, and received unclear, ineffective messages?

Execution is the ability to implement the strategy or the initiative. It is key to demonstrate our contribution to business results. Without execution, there are no tangible outcomes. Without execution, there is no leadership.

Execution is important at all levels and, to be effective, requires the application of some key principles:

- *Meaning of every initiative*: Executives need to understand the "why" of every initiative and communicate its objective and the driving reasons. Without clarity, the executives will be able to effectively neither engage nor lead their team.
- *Communication*: This plays an essential role in engaging, connecting, and moving together toward a common goal. Communication may vary depending on the audience and phase of the initiative, but will always convey a message about the *why* of the initiative and the *what* the executive expects, and can do to help others achieve their goals.

  To be effective, communication must be *simple, short, clear, regular,* and *repeated several times*. This removes possible ambiguity, misunderstanding, and confusion. It creates the expectation for receiving an update at regular times in a certain manner and guarantees everyone has no further doubts or questions about the initiative.
- *Simplicity of actions*: Every initiative must be complemented by an action plan to guarantee its execution in the best possible way. The simpler and more intuitive the actions are, the easier it will be to explain them and ask people to execute them. Let's remember that a complex action can always be simplified and broken down into the sum of simple actions!

- *Rule of 40–70*: Executives need to take action when they have analyzed more than 40% but less than 70% of the available information. Taking a decision before having considered at least 40% of the information exposes to the risk of not having understood the problem well enough. Going over 70%, on the other hand, means trying to define a theoretically perfect approach, but risking that others will seize the opportunity before us. Once the action has started, it will still be possible and necessary to observe its effectiveness and make any corrections.

- *Prioritization of actions*: This must consider impacts (benefits and risks) and associated efforts of proposed actions. Sometimes small, short-term actions (*quick wins*) have big returns. Prioritizing them allows us to gain visibility, engagement, and confidence in the success of the overall initiative. If risks are associated with one action, it will be necessary to prepare a risk mitigation plan and be ready to respond to challenges in case they happen. Both the action prioritization and the risk mitigation plans must be discussed with people involved in or impacted by the initiative in the simplest and most intuitive way.

- *Responsibility and delegation*: Executives must keep accountability for strategic, high-level decisions and delegate operative tasks to their team. Therefore, executives will be able to effectively and efficiently spend their time and efforts on the *big picture*, intervening in the project operations only if and when necessary. Their team will be delegated and responsible for making it happen. Top-down delegation applies at all levels, but with different responsibilities based on seniority and areas of action. For example, consider a team of teams. The executive will delegate to the direct reports and each manager will keep the responsibility for the overall task leveraging on their collaborators for accomplishing the request. In their own way, everyone will be responsible for a "piece" of the execution. Teams will also be accountable to bottom-up feedback their manager and then executive if new challenges emerge and may affect the high-level initiative or strategy. This enables a trust-based, bilateral communication, and finally an effective execution where everyone does and is responsible for tasks based on role and experience.

- *Debrief and continuous improvement:* Executives should celebrate successes and always reflect on lessons learnt when the initiative is over. The leader's mission is to strengthen the team's growth mindset, identifying best practices to reuse and new strategies to avoid past mistakes. Debriefing with all the team creates connection and strengthens the natural bond which generates from having experienced something together.

Figure 11.1 Ability to execute

Credits: Sebastiano Boni

CHAPTER 12

New Board Review

Thanks to Kamila's efficiency, and also to the new collaboration within the team, the project is now running at full capacity.

The conflict with Elisabeth belongs to the past. The same goes for James' demotivation: He is now fully engaged.

The phone rings: It's Andrew.

"Hi Katherine, how are you?"

"Fine, thanks, and you?"

"Pretty well, pretty well... look, the CEO just called me. He would like your new presentation at the next board meeting, which is 2 weeks away."

"Perfect! Thanks for the opportunity. Is there anything in particular that the board wants to review?"

"Be prepared at 360 degrees, but their specific interest is to hear the feedback you are receiving from the various countries."

"Alright. If that's okay with you, do I start preparing right away and can I share a draft with you early next week?"

"Yes, thank you, I would appreciate it very much. I'm in the office on Monday and that would be fine. In the meantime, I am sending you a presentation that was recently given to the board and that was particularly well received. Maybe there is something in the setting that you can reuse."

Another great opportunity to gain visibility for herself and for the good work that the team is doing. This time her presentation will be impeccable.

After a few minutes, the document promised by Andrew arrives in her inbox. It is actually a great piece of work. It is just over a dozen pages, so fluid and intuitive that Katherine can follow their flow simply by looking at them and reading their titles. A full-bodied appendix, full of numbers and tables, completes the document.

"These slides can travel alone," thinks Katherine. She believes that most of the time, even the interesting presentations lose much of their effectiveness when they are sent over e-mail and not presented. But in fact, a good presentation should speak for itself, so that it can be effectively spread across the company without spending too much time. Especially if it is related to a transformation project, where it is important that everyone is on board to drive the change.

She calls up the team and they get to work right away for the new review. The team's "stage director," James, will continue to deal with the overall storytelling, with the help of Mark and Maurice. Elisabeth will lead all the data collection and analysis.

Together, they will try to address Andrew's criticisms, when he described the previous presentation as "all a bit generic."

Last time Andrew also said that "It wasn't clear if you had a proposal... I'm sure if I ask the attendees what they remember about your presentation, they won't be able to answer." So, they will put a special focus on the assertiveness of the tone.

The presentation-example that Andrew gave her is signed by a certain Sandeep Johri, of the company's strategy office. He lives in London; it would take too much time to go visit him, but Katherine pings him for a short video call, to see if he has any advice.

He has, indeed. Sandeep is very kind; he has a thick and very well trimmed beard that inspires calm and confidence. He is happy to take all her questions: "Absolutely Katherine. I follow some rules which I learned in my first years when I was a consultant and that I have consolidated over the years. The first rule is to illustrate your point by referring to 1 or 2 management models that have been created by great management gurus. I am thinking of Ansoff's 2 × 2 matrix or Michael Porter's value chain or Beer and Nohria's E&O theory or others."

"Why are they important?"

"These models have at least 2 big advantages: First they are extremely well thought out and then they are very well known. There is a very high probability that your audience, especially if it is the board, will know them. So, you don't have to make any effort to explain the logic, but you can concentrate only on what is important and that is how you applied that logic to your problem."

"I get it."

"Yes, and of these, there are full libraries, I can send you some links. You will see that eventually, you will find some, maybe a dozen, maybe fewer, that are more congenial to you. Sometimes, when I have to illustrate a situation, a problem, or an opportunity, I quickly go through the list of my favorite models and I choose the most suitable one to represent it."

"This probably also helps you to think, or see the problem from other points of view?"

"Absolutely yes. One thing, however; don't get too carried away: Use only 1 or 2 strategic, managerial models in the same presentation. Too many models would confuse your audience."

"What if I find a good model, but that doesn't represent all aspects of the problem?"

"To decide, use another golden rule of consulting: the 80–20 rule. Almost always, literally in nature, it is 20% of the causes that produce 80% of the effects. This principle was developed by an Italian mathematician, a certain Pareto, more than a hundred years ago."

"I remember the name. I studied his rule at the university."

"Obviously you have to get the right 20%. So, the rule is simple, but it requires a lot of analysis to apply it correctly. By the way, you can also use it effectively to counter some objections. For example, if someone asks you why you have not considered certain secondary aspects, the 80–20 rule gives you the basis for saying 'Yes, thank you, it is a good point, but from the analysis that we have done, this aspect affects the result only by few decimal percentage points.'"

"Yes, it happens to receive these objections from time to time: They can sway a good discussion and shift the attention to marginal details."

"Exactly. I'll give you 2 more tips. The first one is called MECI."

"MECI?"

"It means Mutually Exclusive, Collectively Exhaustive. It is especially important if you speak to a very analytical audience, people like me, for example, who deal with data analysis day in and day out, or people who come from Finance, such as the CFO. This principle is useful when mapping the situation or problem because it shows that you have considered all aspects and taken each one only once, without overlaps."

"Ok, so a MECE analysis organizes all the elements of the problem and does so without duplication?!"

"Exactly. For example, if I segment a population putting all teenagers on one side and people with blue eyes on the other side, this is obviously not a MECE separation because I am excluding all other age groups and all teenagers with different eye colors. This is a trivial example, but when applied to complex situations, the MECE test helps you break down problems into logical and clear groups that you can then tackle individually. In practice, it allows you to break a big question into many smaller problems, whose solutions can then be put back together to show the solution of the original problem."

"Very interesting. You said 2 more pieces of advice. Which is the other one?"

"Prepare 'talking slides,' I mean slides that are clear enough without the need for you to explain them. Try to address only one point for each slide, with the information arranged simply and possibly visually, like with a graphic. Above all, use the title that emphasizes the key point that you want to convey, as opposed to describing what's on the slide."

"I do not understand."

"Let's say that at some point you have a slide with the world map where you show the sales trend over the last 3 years. The title could be 'Sales trend in the last 3 years', very correct, nothing to object… but you would deliver a very different impact if the title were 'USA sales equal to 70% of the growth of the last 3 years,' assuming that this is the message that you want to send across."

"Ah, very clear now. You have been very kind, Sandeep, remember to send me the links you promised."

"It will be done. Good luck with your presentation."

"Touching wood!"

The other thing that Katherine wants to do this time around is to repeat her speech at least 6 times.

James told her that great actors and speakers rehearse at least 20 times! But let's start with 6. At first, she thought it was silly to her: She perfectly knows the content, it's her project. But then she understood that it is not a question of learning the speech by heart: It would come across as artificial and too stiff, discouraging questions or objections. Instead, the point of multiple rehearsals is of acquiring fluency, precision in the use of words, and self-confidence.

This time she has no doubts. She is investing a lot of energy to prepare the review, but it is not wasted time: It will be the seal of their work and a turning point for the company strategy.

Deep Dive—C-Level Presentation

Presenting to C-levels, the CEO's first line, implies:

- Dealing with limited times (about 30 minutes)
- Having an objective typically aimed at supporting a decision or approving an action
- Using PowerPoint to support communication
- Responding to the audience's presentation style expectations typically influenced by the Top Management Consulting firms

Facing these conditions, *preparation* remains the main successful strategy. Preparation means following the best practices of effective communication, focusing on the goal to achieve, identifying the big idea to "sell," studying the audience: their needs, their beliefs, and the level of knowledge that they have already on the topic. Preparation also includes several *role-plays* to practice with the presentation and ensure fluidity in exposures (see Figure 12.1).

The presentation structure follows the rules of the classic storytelling, integrated with some more recent neuroscience and communication studies (see Table 12.1).

Out of the previous structure, it is good to highlight 2 points:

- The *introduction (Situation + Complication)* must include only well-known information. The goal is to set the context, provoke the need, and move quickly to the second part of the structure without either objections or criticisms from the interlocutors.

Figure 12.1 C-level presentation: ideate, study the audience, perform

Credits: Sebastiano Boni

- The *"answer first" approach* of the second part of the structure wants to address the solution to the problem first, then explain its validity (why?) and the ways to implement (how?), and possibly provide other details (What? Who?). This is feasible only if the situation and the approach are set clear and shared upfront. In addition, this has the advantage of anticipating conclusions responding to the typically impatient audience.

Table 12.1 Presentation structure

	Structure	Time frame	Slides
	Introduction	**5%**	**5%**
Situation	As is		
Complication	Description of the problem that generates the need		
Question	Question triggered by the problem and answered by the proposed solution		
	Core of the presentation	**45%**	**45%**
Solution	Proposed solution		
Arguments to support the solution	Answer to "Why is the solution needed?"		
Details to explain how it will be implemented	Answer to "How is the solution implemented?"		
Details to explain who, what, what impacts	Answer to "What can support the implementation? What impacts?"		
	Discussion and Q&A	**40%**	**NA**
	Wrap up and next steps	**10%**	**10%**
TOTAL		30 min	10–15

Once the structure has been prepared, we move on to creating the slides. These must comply with standards, structure, and rules to be effective:

- *Slide*
  - Each slide must convey *only 1 message* to avoid confusion and redundancy.

- ○ Taken as a whole, the slides must comply with the *MECE principle (mutually exclusive, collectively exhaustive)*—every slide has to present 1 message without overlapping with other slides' messages and, overall, the slide deck has to ensure the completeness of the communication.
- *Title*
  - ○ Better if "*talkative,*" stating the main message of the slide.
  - ○ *Standard length* (maximum 2 lines) for all slides (avoid slides with titles of different length or too long!).
- *Contents*
  - ○ *Messages*: It is necessary to carefully select and calibrate only the messages that are important to our audience, avoiding superfluous or nondifferentiating information.
  - ○ *Visual communication*: Each slide must present a graphic or a concept because the brain processes images 60,000 times faster[1] than words and memorizes them more easily. It follows that it is very useful to create a library of frequently used images, with useful graphics to represent strategic models (e.g., Ansoff's 2 × 2 matrix, Kay's triangle), operational tasks (e.g., roadmaps, action plans), conceptual insights (e.g., Venn diagrams, Lego blocks), and infographics.
- *Use of words*: The written slides should be used only when there is no graphic that can better summarize them.
  - ○ They must be chosen with academic rigor and limited to the smallest number possible to ensure synthesis and effectiveness. Super dense slides written in font 10 or below should be banned as they make the pages more like a book to read than a presentation to share.
  - ○ They follow corporate stylistic standards: Every company has its own style guide, and executives must comply with it. Please avoid being creative and follow corporate rules, for example, bold for imported keywords or messages, italics for foreign words, citations, or titles of articles/books/publications.

---

[1] There are many sources for the 60,000 times faster stat. The original source comes from Michael Gazzaniga (1992) and Allen Newell (1990), as cited by the SAGE Handbook of Political Communication, 2012, via Amazon.

- *Bullet points*: The use of bullet points is recommended to give a graphic appearance to words.
  - They must be limited to the maximum number of 6 for facilitating the brain to remember them.
  - They must have the *same format* in terms of length and grammatical structure (e.g., all must start with a verb or noun and a mix of both is to be avoided).
  - They must be *coherent in conceptual terms* (e.g., they can be lists of results or lists of actions, never a mix of both).
- *So what?*: Each slide must include the implication (so what) of the message shared in the slide.

Once the presentation is ready, try to reread it with the eyes and ears of an inexperienced person. If it seems understandable, fluid, and almost intuitive, you passed the litmus test and can be sure that you have prepared an effective presentation.

CHAPTER 13

Debrief With the Team

The presentation to the board went very well. At the end, Andrew left the boardroom with her, this time just to congratulate her. And there was no need: It was clear that everything had gone very well.

It was clear from the questions, all precise and curious.

Sandeep's advice was invaluable and channeled the discussion exactly on the tracks that Katherine wanted.

James' help was also fundamental. More tension toward the desired solution and more dramatization of the problem have turned into a greater emotional engagement of the board, which slowly felt part of a journey, a climb toward the goal. So much so that the board began to use mountain terminology and the CEO defined the results achieved so far as "Apold's new base camp" and this expression immediately began to circulate.

Katherine decides it's time to take stock. She takes a sheet of paper and writes down the moments in which the project has made a leap forward and those in which it has had a setback. She has always done this little personal exercise: It helps her to consolidate ideas and learn from experience.

As the first point, she writes: collaboration.

Then she thinks about it and adds "trust": That is the real prerequisite.

Then on the side, she writes "Design Thinking," which has opened new ways of thinking and seeing the problem, together with "business acumen."

Then "feedback." Andrew's feedback in their first review was harsh, but Katherine had to admit that he was right. And it was a good thing that they had that discussion at the beginning of the project when the work was still very fluid. Thanks to Andrew, the project now stands out for the excellent balance between customer perspective and feasibility.

Then she writes "purpose" and connects it with "team" and "business acumen," because without meaning there is no achievement or success. Without a passionate and involved team, the results are certainly lower.

The road is still long, but the results are now tangible. Kamila's organizational skills have been fundamental. Her reliability and clarity made everyone's job easier and above all made it possible to connect the project to ever wider circles of stakeholders.

It is crystal clear why in their first conversation Kamila had insisted so much on communication: It required effort, but once set it has been a great accelerating factor for the project. It helped show the value, build consensus, and receive contributions that Katherine and the team could never have otherwise.

Katherine is happy and proud of how the attitude of the team members has changed, of how now they are all enthusiastic, optimistic, and engaged.

Once the collaboration had been established in the team, it was easy to exploit each one's strengths. To achieve this, diversity within the team was very important. At the beginning it seemed like a disadvantage: too many different points of view, too many irreconcilable approaches, different backgrounds... instead, the trust that little by little has been established has allowed them to express themselves and confront productively, to see an opportunity in uncertainty, and experiment with new ways. Diversity went beyond the boundaries of Katherine's team and embraced other teams, from Production to Purchasing, to Sales, becoming the real strength of the project.

In the next team meeting, she will dedicate the first 20 minutes to celebrate their success with the team. The result is the fruit of everyone's work and Katherine knows that it is also her legacy: Each member of the team will bring this experience to future projects.

Boston, Friday, November 9, 2020.

Appendix 1

Interviews

We asked 3 leaders to tell us about their professional journey, their experience, and the drivers of their success.

In the following pages, you will find the outcomes of these conversations. They spoke about the importance of people, the need to express their purpose, determination, mindset, and much more.

We let you read and reflect on these testimonies which hopefully will inspire your future actions.

Andrea Cardillo—A Life Dedicated to Coaching

Managing Director Italia, Board Member, Former Chairman of TPC Leadership. Executive and Team Coach (ICF MCC)

Q: As an executive coach with global experience, how widespread is coaching in the business world?

A: It depends on how we define coaching. For the International Coach Federation (ICF), coaching is "a partnership with clients in a thought-provoking and creative process that inspires them to maximize their personal and professional potential.[1]" It is based on a relationship of trust that enables the partnership between the coach and the coachee and allows the coachee to explore new perspectives, stepping out of their comfort zone. In this model, the role of the coach is to facilitate the coachees' reflection, develop their awareness, and support the identification of actions aimed at achieving their objectives. The coach does not suggest, advise, or interpret, but facilitates the reflective, nondirective processes, mainly through powerful questions and active listening.

Considering this definition, the knowledge of coaching is much stronger in the Anglo-Saxon countries (the United States, England, Australia) and in Northern Europe than in the rest of Continental Europe and, in general, in the rest of the world (e.g., Africa, Asia, South America).

However, the ICF definition is not the only one. Other definitions refer to coaching as the broader and more inclusive art of facilitating the development of performance, learning, and personal development. This embraces different approaches ranging from mentoring to coaching. Then, the knowledge of coaching is for sure more widespread if we consider the non-ICF definition.

Moreover, there is an uneven use of the term coaching within organizations. Outside the Human Resources Department (HR), other functions typically associate coaching with giving instructions to direct reports and eventually mentoring them.

This highlights a great, currently unexplored opportunity: to provide people managers with coaching tools to interact, facilitate relationships,

---

[1] ICF Code of Ethics. Part 2. https://coachfederation.org/code-of-ethics (09 Jan 2021)

and increase engagement, performance, and the ability to manage change by visioning, exploring options, and leading the transformation.

Q: Following up on your last tip, how much is coaching really integrated into the corporate culture? How much is it applied?

A: It is difficult to give a single answer to your question. I believe that there are few companies where a true culture of coaching is already present. There are much more companies that have the objective of developing a coaching culture or that offer coaching sessions to the first-line reports or teach some coaching techniques to managers in the hope that they apply or pass them on to their teams, but always in the absence of a true, organic culture of coaching.

"Being a coach" or "coaching" appear more and more often as a required skill for managers. However, the performance evaluation systems for managers do not always reward those who invest more in the development and engagement of people. Most MBOs focus only on business results or, at most, assign a secondary role to measure the managers' impact on the development and the climate of their teams.

Better evaluation systems should measure the levels of engagement, the quality of the relationships between the managers and the employees, and the levels of trust necessary to express an opinion even if critical.

To date, there are still few companies that have integrated upward feedback (i.e., the feedback from reports to the manager) or other 360 feedback systems; even fewer are those that replace quantitative with qualitative assessments and focus on the continuous exchange of feedback between managers and teams to support the continuous learning.

However, the good news is that HR departments are increasingly aware of the impact of managerial behaviors on corporate performance and culture and many started courageously and innovatively experimenting with the integration of a true coaching culture.

Q: What is the critical success factor for an executive, both professionally and personally?

A: It is difficult to define a single success criterion. I believe, however, that a fundamental and common factor in every context is emotional or social intelligence, meaning the ability to read social dynamics (e.g., internal dynamics of a team), build relationships, and make socially intelligent decisions. More mature people in this sense can do 3 things well.

First, they have high self-awareness, that is, they know how to recognize external or internal situations (e.g., their beliefs) that influence their emotional state and their actions. Self-reflection leads to recognizing and managing emotions, stimulates thinking out of the box, and develops lateral thinking.

Second, they know how to "undress" their own point of view to be able to dress in that of others, also interpreting undisclosed emotional needs or states. In this way, they enrich their own "map" of reality with those of others, which leads them to make decisions that are more balanced, inclusive, and aware of impacts on the system of their stakeholders.

Third, they have the systemic ability to recognize the way in which business systems/processes impact relational dynamics, behaviors, choices, and corporate culture. Structures influence behaviors and these, repeated over time, create a culture.

Q: What is the role of the search for one's own purpose or the sense that guides professional self-realization?

A: Purpose varies at each stage of life. Age shifts one's point of view from "I" to "we," from the individual to the role that the individual has in the system. The concept of systems evolves and becomes broader and broader embracing the team, the organization, the community, and so on.

Our perspective becomes more and more inclusive and the purpose expands year after year. Questions turn from "Who do I want to be?" to "What impact do I want to have?" to "What is a successful life for me?" to "What legacy do I want to leave?"

Purpose is also important in corporate strategies because it has a direct impact on the quality of the relationships that a company establishes with all internal and external stakeholders. We create engagement and we are measured on the level of consistency between what we say and do, on the *why* and on the *how* we can achieve it.

The organizations which are most effective in creating engagement are those in which it is easy for the individuals to find a connection between personal and corporate purpose. Here, coaching makes a difference.

Instead, in highly evolving and highly complex scenarios, organizations typically forget the big purpose and focus on micro-objectives (e.g., initiatives aimed at achieving the quarterly goal), losing the connection with the purpose and with the *why* and *for whom* we do what we do.

As a consequence, one of the characteristics of the most successful executives is their ability to energize others by reinforcing the *why* and *how* we do what we do and so increase people's motivation (e.g., I don't work for earning money, but I work because I know I do something that makes a difference, I know I am a good model for my children and my community).

Q: How many people reflect on their personal purpose and then work with purpose at an organizational level?

A: The question about the meaning of our life is a question we all have. It becomes more and more pressing as the time passes and we have less time to live. It is an ethical question, which science cannot answer. I believe that the real challenge is that the answer is not given or cannot be found on the outside. Even when we choose an answer from a religious or spiritual authority, we are still responsible for choosing that answer.

Many people prefer to repress this question because it is difficult to answer without really confronting one's responsibilities.

Similar dynamics are amplified in the workplace. For this reason, the investigation and definition of the purpose are becoming an increasingly urgent issue. My experience is that today more than ever, employees and customers look at the way the organization reflects, responds, and addresses the question related to its purpose. This seems to be even more true for the new generations.

Q: What are the critical factors for establishing effective relationships with the network of people (team, peer, boss, and so on) executives interact with daily?

A: It is to honestly admit when they do not know. We all feel the pressure of always having the right answers to take the decision that makes everyone happy. This, however, is a recipe for disaster.

When things change and there are so many variables at play, a person cannot have all the answers. In my experience, it is better to admit that we do not have all the answers and to involve others in finding the solutions, cocreating together with the best response to a situation of uncertainty.

This is founded and is based on a healthy relationship of mutual trust and on the coresponsibility of people. Equal relationships are created between adults: Managers are no longer in a parental situation in which they have all the answers for their team and collaborators in that of the children waiting for the manager to have all the answers for them.

Q: In the current situation of uncertainty and strong change, what approach/strategy would you, as a coach, implement to face this change?

A: Listen to what is emerging, because the answers from the past may no longer work. In other words, adopting a bifocal view, taking time to digest what is happening now while keeping in the background the opportunities that emerge from the change.

Careful observation and emotional intelligence highlight problems, but also opportunities. They allow us to connect with emotions, digesting and managing them to make conscious decisions according to our purpose and our values, without being at the mercy of the fear of change. Being in authentic contact with our emotions and intuitions allows us to hoist the anchor and navigate the sea of uncertainty with greater freedom.

Q: Our interview has come to the end, would you like to add something else?

A: Yes, I would like to reinforce the need for a connection between purpose and business strategies.

The more scenarios are uncertain, the more difficult it is to plan, predict, identify unique relationships between action and response of the system. I believe that in the next few years we will see organizations increasingly exploring inside-out strategies starting from their sense of purpose and values and not just from the outside-in search for existing market niches. These organizations are the ones that will truly shape the environment around them in an integrated, forward-looking, and sustainable way.

Maria Letizia Mariani—A Leader with Purpose

Chief Marketing and Strategy Officer, Head of Division Conventional Products, and Board Member Signify. Board Member Prysmian Group.

Q: Letizia, what are the 2 things you would like to say to aspiring executives?

A: This is a very difficult question because there are billions of them, but for me, 2 are particularly important.

The first is not to try to be perfect. Because perfection is a narcissistic need. At the same time, never give up on being authentic and coherent.

For me, being authentic is to be generous enough to put our specificity and diversity at the service of society. Coherent means being in harmony with what you ask of others, therefore "lead by example." This is my first suggestion.

The second is that leadership is a responsibility. It is not a role, it is not status, it is not a title, but it is responsibility. In particular, the responsibility we take toward others, their development, their involvement, their health, and ultimately their success.

We must be conscious of this responsibility, we must handle it with care and dedication, which means an investment of quality time from us.

As in sport, you need to have passion. Talent helps, but you become a champion only if you practice and train hard.

So my message to aspiring young executives is to prepare to work hard. Prepare to take responsibility and be conscious of it.

Q: In your career, you have made many choices. Which of these was the most important?

A: First of all, I have to say one thing, even at the cost of sounding a little naïve: For me, a career has never been a goal.

The family environment I come from was foreign to corporate life and I came across it a little by chance. I have never seen the career as a personal ambition: For me, it has always been important to look for things that make me grow, that stimulate and intrigue me.

I had a fairly heterogeneous education: In high school, I studied Latin and ancient Greek, then at university, I studied science, then I threw myself into computer science, but keeping the passion for literature, which comes from my family.

For me, connections have always been the most valuable thing: I feel pleasure when I can find a common thread between different areas, a connection, a similarity, and an influence.

By natural inclination, at work, I have always looked for growth and new stimuli that would allow me to satisfy my curiosity rather than think in terms of career as an end in itself.

I remember, for example, when my boss told me that I had been promoted to Director. He said it to me as if it were an enormous leap and it was, but I reacted quite neutrally and, unintentionally, I disappointed him: I did not see it was a fundamental step from my system of values. A higher degree of seniority is something that pleases for 2 days. When you get an important promotion like, for example, the appointment to vice-president, everyone congratulates you for a couple of days, but then you are alone with yourself.

Instead, it is what you do every day that must bring you the energy and passion to get up every morning, go, and dedicate the day to the service of something. If that something is a business card, you are making poor use of your life. Conversely, if that something gives you a strong sense of satisfaction, it fulfills your purpose, and then it makes sense.

A very important choice in my career was when I turned down a position as vice-president for a control job at the European level. I did so because the role made no sense compared to what I liked and wanted to do; it was far from my interests and I did not feel I could bring value or grow.

I rejected the offer and, for this decision, I was considered "out of place," a fish out of the water, not exactly sane. The common thought in the company, in fact, is that, if you are not vice-president and you are offered a position as vice-president, you do not even ask what you are going to do: You accept simply because it is an important promotion.

For me, however, the fundamental and discriminating factor for choosing a new job has always been the activity I have to do every day and its alignment with my personal purpose. If it is not aligned, then it does not make sense to me, regardless of the job title.

Refusing this offer was the best choice because other opportunities have opened up that are perfectly in line with my sense of work, which I like and which make me grow.

Q: Even if it was not your goal, you actually had a great career. Which decision has advanced your career the most?

A: More than a single fact, I would say an attitude. It has always come naturally to me to look at the collective interest, the greater good.

Whatever I do, I frame it in a broader perspective and this, not immediately, but over the distance, has paid off because I have always been seen as a person who is capable of representing the company.

It comes naturally to me to put things in perspective and give priority to the higher interest over the individual one.

I learned this from one of my former bosses who used to say he was "a manager of the company, on loan to the Services Division." First of all, he felt, rightly so, a manager of the company, in its entirety. This way of seeing enabled him to put any choice into perspective. It is like saying: right now, I have a certain responsibility, but this is instrumental to a greater responsibility, which is that collectively we have to bring the company to success.

I find this point of view very beautiful and it has always been my natural and instinctive way of thinking, but I rationalized it after observing and listening to this manager.

I think this attitude is the factor that has helped me most in my career, in the sense that most of the steps I took were offered to me because I had this attitude.

Q: The spirit of service?

A: Yes, exactly. The spirit of service that you see in practice in so many actions and decisions.

Some people only look at KPIs (key performance indicators) and their sole purpose becomes to reach these KPIs.

But KPIs are not the real goal; KPIs are simply a way to measure some things. The real purpose must be higher: how to serve customers and contribute to the growth of the organization.

Some people attach themselves to certain KPIs and distort the ultimate sense of the organization, sometimes even going astray. It is like confusing the end with the means.

As an example, take Operations. If, for instance, the goal is to reduce inventory, there are many ways to do so, from the dumbest to the most structured.

If you want to achieve this goal in a given quarter, it is not difficult: Just reduce the inventory of the products with the highest turnover. This way, in the corporate dashboard, your performance is "green," but clearly, you have created a sales problem for the next quarter.

In other words, sometimes the desire to do well risks leading us astray by losing the true sense of what we are responsible for.

The real goal is to drive efficiently and effectively a complex machine so that customers are always served, without creating obsolescence in the product portfolio and inventory. This is always more complex than what can be expressed by a single KPI and this systemic perspective must be cultivated and encouraged because it can really make a difference.

Q: It requires a certain degree of maturity...

A: That is right: It requires a certain maturity and balance. It does not mean that achieving your goals is not important; on the contrary, this is fundamental.

However, it is necessary to achieve them by targeting the overall interest and to understand and accept that some indicators may not be green if this is functional to another higher objective.

Q: A boss of mine used to say, "It's good to be focused on KPIs until you don't become KPI blind."

A: That is right, the concept is exactly that. I could not express it better. While we easily see the problem when we meet nongoal-focused people, it is harder to recognize early on the potential harm that comes from goal-obsessed people.

Q: In your wonderful career, you have for sure also made mistakes. Can you tell us something that you would do differently if you could go back?

A: I have made a lot of mistakes in my career, but one, in particular, has been a great lesson for me.

It dates back to several years ago when I was doing synchronized swimming and I started coaching a team at a club in Rome.

The club had 2 teams: one more junior, which I coached, and one more senior, led by my former coach and my point of reference.

It was my first coach experience and I felt honored to lead a team.

My team was made up of girls within the same age range, between 12 and 14 years old, plus a much younger girl, perhaps 8 years old, a little frail, with less confidence in the water. By chance, her name was also Letizia, like me.

At the end of the year, there was an essay, it was not just a performance, but also a competition between clubs, with scores and a winner.

It was up to me to decide the selection that would participate and I was uncertain whether to include Letizia.

I asked for help from my former coach, I explained my doubt to her and she replied that being my team, I had to decide.

After a night tormented by doubts, I decided not to put her on the team.

The competition went very well and my team won. But I made a mistake and I realized that the very moment I told Letizia that she would not be on the team. I saw in her eyes that my choice was wrong.

I then tortured myself and wondered why I did so. Did I do so for the others? Or did I do it for myself? It was my first year as a coach, I wanted to prove that I could do the best performance, and I knew that with her we would hardly have won.

I made the wrong choice because I chose the thing that served my personal goal, without thinking about what my true purpose was: to train and develop the girls, give them opportunities, recognize the path of a young athlete who had put a lot of effort and had grown up.

This mistake taught me a lot. First of all, I learned from my coach, who had the courage to make me wrong. If she had told me "Of course you have to put her in," I would not have learned anything. Unfortunately,

I learned at the cost of the pain I created for this little girl. If I could go back, I'd like to apologize.

I realized the influence I had on other people's lives. I had the responsibility of building a person and I failed in this task.

I was wrong, but I learned the fundamental thing, which is that you have to make friends with mistakes: You have to recognize them, admit them, and learn.

Mistakes are the biggest support for our development. Even if admitting them is exhausting.

Q: This is even truer at work...

A: Absolutely. Hence, the sense of responsibility that is fundamental for me. When you are leading a group, in any form or discipline, be it in sport or work, you take on a responsibility and when you take on a responsibility, you have to forget about yourself. The theme is no longer you, it is not about you, it is about what you make available to others and how you are able to create the conditions for that team and for those people to give their best.

This is your responsibility and it has a real impact on people. For good and unfortunately also for bad. You see the impact every day.

It is very important for me to listen and be close to people.

Then difficult choices come, like the times when you have to reduce the organization. You have to always do it with respect and transparency, with attention to people, try to be close, do not think about yourself, but think about what you are doing and what it means for others, for the company, for the customers, for the organization.

If you can put others first, generally you make the right decisions.

Q: Tell us now about a setback, an ambition that you had, and for which they chose another person. How did you react and how did you come out stronger than before?

A: I said that I did not have a career idea, but then when you are inside the mechanism and look around you, you see things you would like to do. You must know that I have run 3 times for the same position and for 3 times I was told no.

It has been an interesting journey: The first time I was not ready; the second time I had the right profile, but there was a candidate stronger than me; the third time I was probably overqualified for that role.

The first time I was so convinced that they were going to give me the job that I did not bother showing much interest, without reflecting on the fact that those who choose hardly assign a position to a person who does not show the desire to take it. I think that was why they did not choose me, but I took it very badly. Really bad: I reacted by giving air to all my frustration, going around telling the interview panel that they had made the wrong choice, taking it personally.

I did not ask questions, I just let off steam, which is so wrong.

The second time was easier because I recognized the value of the person who had been chosen in my place. When you recognize that the person who has been chosen in your place is of value, with characteristics that you do not have, different or better, and from whom you can learn, it is easier to get over it.

The third time I took it with philosophy because by then I was no longer really interested in that job, I applied for a spirit of service, because I was convinced that I could make a difference at that moment, even if I believed I had outgrown the requirements for the role. So I thought "worse for you": I would have given more than I would have learned. However, knowing that I was rejected hurt me the third time too.

What I have learned in this series of failures is that after a failure you must first digest it. Take the time to cool off and then face the situation in a constructive spirit, which means asking questions to understand what was not adequate, what was lacking in my professional experience, or what had not been considered.

You have to have this dialogue when you are calm, to avoid attacking and triggering defensive mechanisms in the counterpart. You must have the ability to take the person or persons who were on the selection committee, ask, and listen and listen again. Then you learn a lot because you understand what you have to do to improve yourself or to make others see things that are there, but that you could not convey.

The most valuable principle in all of this is that you must not act like the victim. When you have a setback, the simplest thing is to think that you have been discriminated against and find a justification external to you, which justifies you.

On the contrary, not playing the victim is essential. We choose the roles to play and if we choose to play the victim, then we become a victim.

In reality, there is always something to learn, something that you could or should have done differently and, if you manage to grasp that point, then Mandela was really right when he said that "I never lose: Either I win or I learn."

It is a painful journey and, for me, "digestion" is the most important part. If I do not wait to have "digested" the defeat and immediately seek feedback, I am vulnerable and, by defense, I become aggressive.

First, I have to calm down, I have to distance myself, and then look for the feedback that always becomes a huge source of teaching to work on.

Q: So asking with genuine curiosity and not to prove you are right?

A: Exactly. You have to be motivated by the desire to understand what you can do differently, what you can do to improve yourself.

In the end, anything is our choice.

If you work on it, eventually you will be ready for something great. This is what happened to me: I found myself in front of an opportunity and I was ready, thanks to what I had learned and applied.

Then there is always a bit of luck too. In my case, I crossed paths with a company that strongly believes in the value of innovation, sustainability, and diversity, all topics that fascinate me.

Luck must also be helped. As Arnold Palmer, one of the greatest golfers in history, said, "How strange, the more I train the more fortunate I become."

If you lack the ingredients, it is difficult for a nice dessert to come out even though you may have the best oven available.

When you arrive in a well-equipped kitchen you must have all your ingredients with you; you must have seen soufflé with a regal bearing coming out of your hands, but also sadly limp cakes. You must have the humility to continue learning and a great desire to serve excellent dishes.

Then you will feel that you are ready to do well and to live with satisfaction every day of your life.

Marco Airoldi—A Different Perspective

Koinos Capital SGR CEO. Former CEO Benetton Group, former Senior Partner Boston Consulting Group (BCG), former General Manager Autogrill

Q: Marco, let's talk about leadership. You told us you wanted to share an unusual perspective.

A: Yes, I propose that we approach our conversation by talking about how to close a work experience, thus focusing on leaving.

Over the years, I have noticed that many, especially the younger ones, behave with a short time horizon in mind.

As if, leaving a job, they were convinced that they would close a door behind them, forever, and no longer have any contact with that company and those people. This is a serious mistake.

It makes no sense to end a relationship badly; on the contrary I believe it is important to actively engage in trying to end it as best as possible. There is a way to start things right, a way to get things right, and a way to end them well.

Unfortunately, it is almost never taught how to finish them. We only teach how to start them and how to carry them forward.

I would like to tell you how I personally experienced the importance of what I am saying.

I have never tried to finish the various phases of my professional experience well for utilitarian reasons. I did it only because it seemed ethically the right thing to do toward all the people involved: the employer, the customers, the colleagues. But then, as a by-product, I also had a positive return.

The story is as follows: After a few years in BCG, I had reached the threshold of partnership. My promotion had been decided and it was being formalized.

At this point, a customer with whom I had worked very well for years, Autogrill, offered me the Operations Director position.

After the usual ponderings and tribulations, which are always there when it comes to choosing between 2 interesting options, I decided to accept because the challenge of a line role stimulates me.

Obviously, I had some ongoing projects with BCG at the time. In particular, one of these was very demanding, difficult to manage professionally and emotionally (it was a truly massive cost reduction that a multinational urgently needed to operate in its division).

As always happens when you are offered a job, the new employer put pressure on me to start as soon as possible: The old manager was retiring and there was an urgent need to make a good handover.

However, I negotiated to close first the current project with this other client and I managed to move the start date a little further, so that I could finish the project I was responsible for and which I had committed to bring to term.

Therefore, I continue to work at BCG to complete this assignment. The final presentation to the client is scheduled for my last day of work at BCG, a Friday, so that the following Monday I would start at Autogrill.

For an unexpected event by the customer at the last moment, the final presentation must be canceled and moved to the following Monday.

I really wanted to present personally the final report, also for the personal relationship with the client's CEO. So, I start my first day of work at Autogrill asking for a permit. For me it was not conceivable not to participate in the important and delicate final closing meeting of the project.

I then discuss the project on Monday and close it with a very satisfied client. The next day, on Tuesday, I start working at Autogrill.

I enjoy working at Autogrill very much; it was a very nice experience. I deal with the reorganization of Operations in Italy, then I am appointed General Manager Europe, where, through various acquisitions, we build the foundation of the company's international presence. After some years, in 2000, I am caught up in the whirlwind of the Internet and I decide to leave Autogrill to launch, with others, a venture capital fund.

I communicate my intention to leave and this, as it always happens, generates a bit of confusion. Again, I postpone my departure for few months to complete all the most critical projects that were in progress, to leave things in order and do an orderly handover to my successor.

After that, my partners and I start building this fund. It was a leap in the dark, because I had resigned without having a new job and certainly before we had gathered the necessary resources to start the fund.

We therefore begin to structure the fund and look for investors and, quite quickly, we are able to successfully close the fund raising.

Then, however, everything happens. The bursting of the Internet bubble arrives, the attack on the twin towers, everything stops and... we decide that there are no longer the conditions to create the investment vehicle. We therefore block everything and free the investors from their commitment.

After spending more than a year to get the fund started and just as much to "dismantle" it, I find myself having to look for a job.

To my great pleasure, however, I am contacted by my 2 previous employers: BCG and Autogrill.

In the first case to return to the role of Partner and in the other to be the General Manager.

Beyond the personal satisfaction of this, my point here is that both offers were the result of having left well my previous experiences and maintaining good relations.

Let me clarify: I did not "get out" well because I was thinking about returning. On the contrary, for me both chapters had been closed permanently and I had completed my assignments at my best only out of a sense of professional fairness toward the companies and the people I worked with. The way, however, in which I had closed the projects and the working relationships later proved to be useful also from a personal point of view.

Receiving 2 excellent opportunities, simultaneously, from companies to which I had remained very attached also created some embarrassment of choice. Eventually I decided to return to BCG, but with clear and open communication with everyone during the decision process. So much so that Autogrill then hired me as a consultant.

So I return to BCG, at this point as a Partner, and therefore also with the task of bringing new customers—in addition to Autogrill.

It is not a trivial task to rejoin a consulting firm after 7 years, having to rebuild a customer base, obviously with pressure on results.

At this point, another interesting thing happens: A private equity fund has recently made a major acquisition in the food sector and has hired a new CEO.

The choice falls on the former CEO of the division of that multinational company with which I had made my last BCG project before joining Autogrill. In those 7 years, we had not heard from each other again, also because he, in the meantime, had moved to South America.

Then he returns to Italy for his new role and learns that I have returned to BCG. We resume contacts and agree on drafting the business plan.

So, I find myself acquiring a new important customer immediately after returning as a Partner. This has helped me tremendously in my second career at BCG.

Putting all the pieces of the story together, you can see 2 or 3 good examples of how things well done and, above all, well closed are also selfishly useful.

This has also become a selection criterion that I usually use in interviews. When I hire someone, I too would like him or her to start right away, ideally the next morning. One of the things that interests me, however, is whether the people I choose are able to leave by closing well the things they had started, without leaving open problems behind them. If they can manage the excitement for the new assignment and the pressure from the new employer without failing in their duties toward the current employer.

Immediate availability gives the new employer a short-term advantage (you have the new employee immediately on board and you can take a problem off your list), but the fact remains that the employee has left open problems behind and may do so again in the future.

To conclude, this story has 2 implications for me. The first is ethical and has to do with how you close things off. The second is that whatever you do, it has a long shadow.

In business, I keep meeting the same people over and over again. Your reputation follows you everywhere.

When you are 25, you are not so aware of it. It seems to you that the world is big, but in reality, it is not.

If you do your job well to the last, in addition to the ethical aspect, you also have a practical advantage: Not only do you do the right thing, you also do what ensures the best return.

Q: How does the "ethical" behavior of closing a work experience link with the issue of trust?

A: You remind me of a book by Robert Axelrod, *The Evolution of Cooperation*, which describes an experiment aimed at finding the best strategy to deal with the prisoner's dilemma.

They assigned different strategies to a number of people (subjects) they had selected for the experiment.

In the experiment, there were more subjects than strategies, so each strategy was applied several times, in repeated encounters. This in order to select the best strategy with a Darwinian logic of natural selection, where the best strategies prevail.

Some strategies were very sophisticated, but, in the end, the winning strategy was very simple and it was named *Tit for Tat*: Cooperate with those who cooperated with you the previous turn. Do not cooperate with those who have not cooperated with you before.

This brings me back to what we said before, that our interactions in business are repeated interactions more often than we imagine. Here is where your trust capital—that you build or destroyed in previous interactions—comes into play.

Q: Marco, some time ago you told me about a question you always ask during interviews. An aspect that you particularly want to check, especially for positions of responsibility.

A: Yes, I remember it well. When you do interviews, people always tell you about the things they did well.

I am interested in asking what went wrong. What was the worst disaster they experienced and how they came out of it.

When you interview someone who just tells you that he has always had the best grades in university, the most brilliant promotions, the fastest advancements... I think it's dangerous to hire him, because I don't know how they would react if they "slipped."

They may melt like a soufflé at the first difficult moment, since they have never had any in life.

For me it is essential that they tell me what their worst moment was, the thing where they found the most difficulties.

Who has never had troubled moments? What matters is how you manage to react when the hard time comes. Not just how good you are at doing the right things. If you arrived at the interview, you did the right things and I somehow found out about it, otherwise we wouldn't be here.

The ability to put the shattered pieces back together, to be able to maintain clarity and resistance to frustration are fundamental skills, once you have acquired your technical and relational skills.

The best salespeople tend also to be the best at managing frustration. The job of a sales rep is one of the most frustrating. They "slam doors in your face" with a high frequency.

Some time ago, I read about an experiment in which they asked swimmers to do a series of laps as quickly as possible, working hard to their limit. Then they didn't tell them the real time they had made, but a somehow worse one and asked them to try again.

The swimmers then divided into 2 groups: those who, knocked down by the poor result that had been communicated (poorer than their perception), performed worse than before and those who, on the other hand, prodded by the negative response, managed to obtain an even better time. Here, I look for this type of swimmer when I hire someone!

Appendix 2

The Science of Happiness

The science of happiness is part of positive psychology and it studies the roots, causes, and implications of our happiness. Nowadays, we think of happiness as a goal to pursue, catch, and guarantee forever. A new car, a beautiful dress, or a vacation are certainly pleasant moments and influence our emotional state. Yet these are expressions of temporary happiness, which researchers call *hedonic happiness*. They are linked to individual pleasure and typically to temporary positive emotions. Long-term happiness is different: It is linked to the pursuit of a goal that transcends our self-interest and embraces a greater purpose. This kind of happiness, named *eudaimonic happiness*, is rooted in our true human origin and provides several clinical benefits: stronger immune system, greater resistance to stress, better cardiovascular functions, better sleep quality, less chance of depression, greater longevity. It is studied more and more as the digital world, the strong competition, and the time pressure increase self-esteem, inequality, and loneliness, and distance individuals from their true nature of prosocial, collaborative, and generous human beings.

The new role of the *Chief Happiness Officer* (CHO) is born with the mandate to ensure employees' happiness and joy. Happy employees, in fact, are better employees: They have higher levels of creativity, productivity, and collaboration; they are more forward looking and tend to embrace change with optimism. Finally, they are more engaged (less risk of resignation) and demonstrate better brand advocacy. The CHO is called upon to bridge the gap between expectations and reality. A survey conducted in 2018 found that 90% of the 500 workers surveyed expect to feel joy at work but only 37% actually do. The good news, however, is that happiness can be developed. Neuroscientific studies have revealed that:

- 40% of the causes of happiness can be managed.
- The brain is a "muscle": It can be trained to develop new abilities (including happiness).

What are the factors that make us happy?

The 3 basic sources of happiness are:

- *Sport*: Physical activity stimulates the production of endorphins and serotonin, known as well-being and happiness hormones, and counteracts stress by reducing the level of cortisol in the blood.
- *Sleep*: Sleeping 8 hours and having a good quality sleep allow the body to recover the energy to better face a new day. Studies link sleep to better physical and mental well-being and to the reduction of stress, anxiety, and depression. Nowadays, our sleep is strongly impacted by the stress associated with uncertain macroeconomic situations, hyper-competitive work environments, and dissatisfaction with the corporate role.
- *Sense*: Contributing to a higher and greater goal, which transcends our self-interest, allows us to connect with others, justify our existence in the name of a greater cause, gaining a sense of fulfillment. This need has its roots in our primordial origin as prosocial beings, who found in the community a safe place to live and raise the little ones.

How can scientific findings be concretely translated into business practice? What are the initiatives that leaders can implement to support the happiness of their collaborators?

- *Limiting the sources of stress*: The World Health Organization (WHO) has defined stress at work as the "health epidemic of the 21st century." WHO associated stress with poor work organization, poor management, and limited collaboration among colleagues. The increasing pressure to do better, do more, and do faster, coupled with the uncertainty of the future, generates errors, stress, burnout with an estimated business cost of $300 billion in 2001 only in the United States. To limit stress, leaders must:
  - *Ensure engaging and satisfying activities for their employees*: WHO has shown that the greatest source of work stress is

working on activities that are not aligned with our abilities. Both hyper-simple, monotonous, unimportant activities and those too challenging for the individual's abilities generate frustration, resentment, and stress. It is up to the leaders to assign engaging and satisfying activities to their collaborators according to their potential and their knowledge. Collaborators should enter into a *state of flow*, which is the intense, rewarding engagement in an activity that brings to lose the sense of time. The flow requires creativity and mental resources, but it brings fulfillment and gratification. People reach the state of flow when they engage in activities that are interesting and challenging, but still feasible relative to their skills and abilities.

○ *Communicate clearly, transparently, and regularly*: Humans do not like uncertainty. It generates doubt, suspicion, fear. They are instinctively driven to seek answers that are not communicated to them, but in doing so they waste energy. Leaders will always have to explain the *why* behind every decision. Taking these clarifications for granted or assuming that employees simply execute what is decided at the top is a huge mistake and generates disengagement.

○ *Provide the team with a peaceful working environment*: The team must be a "safe harbor," a calm environment to work, self-express, and trust colleagues. Leaders must ensure the best possible environment for their teams, filtering the stress that weighs on their shoulders and always maintaining a positive, proactive, and empathetic attitude.

○ *Oppose hyper-perfectionism and waste of time*: Hyper-perfectionism and waste of time (e.g., never-ending meetings) generate discomfort and stress due to the work that accumulates while individuals are busy with other activities. Let's take meetings as an example. A recent article in *The Economists* revealed that 80% of the time of 80% of attendees is wasted. In another analysis, *Doodle* estimated a cost of $399 billion only in the United States due to unnecessary or poorly organized meetings. Leaders must therefore define clear goals, build and stick to the agenda, prepare and limit participation only to necessary people.

- o *Promote an equal work–life balance*: The focus on performance and digitalization pushes to work harder, faster, and under greater pressure. Digitization allows us to be always on, but this wears away the barriers that previously limited the working hours. Work reaches us in the evening, at night, on weekends, and even on vacation. This, of course, creates stress. Leaders must promote a healthy and balanced work style, calibrating the number and sustainability of assignments and avoiding interactions outside working hours. They must also support their collaborators in case of perceived or shared personal complications, possibly leveraging the expert support made available by the company.

- *Sponsor activities with greater than individual purpose*: The generous nature of human beings and the need to give meaning to their life lead to the search for activities that transcend self-interest and create value for others. To mention a few examples, many companies have volunteer programs, others sponsor internal activities in which employees give back their time to support minorities of gender, race, or religion. Leaders have to promote and support these initiatives because they enhance employee experience and increase their happiness. Furthermore, if the experience is shared with other colleagues, it strengthens their bonds and benefits teamwork.

- *Promote intra and extra-team collaboration*: Our prosocial nature must be fulfilled inside and outside the team. Leaders must:
  - o Foster disciplined collaboration within their team, with clear and recognized roles for participants and with a safe environment for the authentic expression of opinions.
  - o Inspire collaboration through example. If leaders' behavior is collaborative, kind, and authentic, this will trigger a virtuous circle which will push the collaborator to emulate it. This is known as the *Tit for Tat* mechanism, where one's behavior is always observed and mirrored.
  - o Create new experiences and learning opportunities through cross-team engagements.

- *Sponsor the benefits of mindfulness* and encourage employees to practice it every day: Mindfulness is the nonjudgmental, moment-by-moment awareness of thoughts, feelings, body sensations, and surrounding environments. The benefits of mindfulness include:
  - ○ Increased focus and concentration on the present activity. Mindfulness also helps manage our brain habit to wander and think about past or future facts (mind wandering). This consciousness makes us recognize the distractions and allows us to quickly return to the present situation, limiting energy waste and stress.
  - ○ Greater empathy and ability to manage emotions. Mindfulness-based stress reduction (MBSR) is the mindfulness method with proven clinical benefits, used in the case of burnout to help people recognize, uncouple, and manage emotions.
  - ○ Greater ability to recognize and appreciate the positive, otherwise little considered micro-moments which give joy and fight stress.
  - ○ Greater creativity and openness to experimentation because mindfulness interrupts the conditioned responses that prevent the exploration of new ideas and sustain change.

  Mindfulness is based on the concept of brain neuroplasticity, which is the possibility of training the brain and developing new habits. The more exercise (mindfulness practice) we do, the more benefits we realize. The employee is always responsible for practicing consistently to obtain the expected benefits.
- *Provoke positive emotions*: Moments of joy, although temporary, generate positivity toward the future and create a better context in which to work and develop the sense of belonging, gratitude, and happiness. Leaders can provoke positive emotions in various ways:
  - ○ Public appreciation of collaborators' achievements or abilities
  - ○ Authentic interest in collaborators as people
  - ○ Support to the collaborators' professional development
  - ○ Sponsorship of mindfulness as a way to catch and appreciate positive micro-moments

Collaborators' happiness will imply a sense of belonging toward the leader, the team, and the company, greater positivity and antifragility, and greater creativity. Developing employee happiness is therefore a win–win–win situation: happier employees mean better-supported leaders and more innovative, productive, agile companies which better face the challenges of the new digital age.

References

Atkinson, M. 2010. *Step-by-Step Coaching*. United States: Exalon Publishing Limited.

Coggan, P. February 06, 2021. "The Lockdown Has Caused Changes Of Routine." *The Economist, Bartleby*. https://economist.com/business/2021/01/13/the-lockdown-has-caused-changes-of-routine.

Csikszentmihalyi, M. 1990. *Flow*. New York, NY: Harper & Row.

Blais, L. January 16, 2012. "Look Past Performance to see Potential." *Diversity Executive*. https://egonzehnder.com/what-we-do/board-advisory/insights/look-past-performance-to-see-potential.

Botsman, R. 2017. *Who Can You Trust? How Technology Brought Us Together—and Why It Could Drive Us Apart*. Great Britain: Penguin Books Limited.

Botsman, R. 2019. "The Currency of Trust." *DLDconference*. https://youtube.com/watch?v=-vbPXbm8eTw (accessed January 16, 2021).

Brown, T. 2009. *Change by design*. New York, NY: Harper Business.

Brun, J.P. 2007. "Work-Related Stress: Scientific Evidence-Base of Risk Factors, Prevention and Costs." *World Health Organization*. https://who.int/occupational_health/topics/brunpres0307.pdf?ua=1 (accessed February 06, 2021).

Burnett, B., and D. Evans. 2018. *Designing Your Life: Build a Life that Works for You*. Great Britain: Vintage.

Dilts, R., T. Hallborm, and S. Smith. 1990. *Beliefs*. Portland: Metamorphous Press.

Doodle. 2018. "Financial Impact of Meetings." https://google.com/url?q=https://meeting-report.com/financial-impact-of-meetings/0&sa=D&source=editors&ust=1612365864859000&usg=AOvVaw2NgB6vOETFuEGBvrlu7oDG" \t "_blank (accessed February 06, 2021).

Duarte, N. 2019. *DataStory*. Canada: Ideapress publishing.

Duarte, N. 2012. "The Secret Structure of Steve Jobs's speech.mp4." *TedX*. https://youtube.com/watch?v=ujYHR9kKA10 (accessed January 17, 2021).

Duarte, N. 2010. *Resonate*. United States of America: John Wiley & Sons. Inc.

Duarte, N. 2008. *Slide:ology*. Canada: O'Reilly.

Dweck, C. 2017. *Mindset*, 2nd ed. London: Robinson.

Estefani, S.E. 2017. *The Power of Meaning – Crafting the Life that Matters*. New York, NY: Crown Publishers.

Gallwey, T. 2016. *The Inner Game of Tennis*. United Kingdom: Pan Books.

Gallwey, T. 2009. *The Inner Game of Stress*. United States: Random House Inc.

Goleman, D. 1996. *Emotional Intelligence*. London: Bloomsbury Publishing PLC.

Goleman, D. 2008. "What Makes a Leader?" *Best of HBR on Emotionally Intelligence Leadership*, 2nd ed. Harvard Business School Publishing Corporation.

Hansen, M. 2018. *Great at work*. UK: Simon & Schuster.

Kabat-Zinn, J. 2020. *Full Catastrophe Living*. London: Piatkus.

Landsberg, M. 2015. *The Tao of coaching*. Great Britain: Profile books.

Lencioni, P. 2002. *The five dysfunctions of a team*. San Francisco: Jossey Bass.

Lindstrom, M. 2016. *Small data*. New York, NY: St.Martin's Press.

Liu, A. 2019. "Making Joy a Priority at Work." *Harvard Business Review*. https://hbr.org/2019/07/making-joy-a-priority-at-work (accessed February 06, 2021).

Lyubomirsky, S. 2008. *The How of Happiness*. USA: Penguin Group.

Maxwell, J.C. 1993. *Developing the Leader Within You*. Nashville: Injoy Inc.

McKee, A. 2017. *To be Happy at Work*. USA: Harvard Business Review Press.

Minto, B. 2009. *The Pyramid Principle*, 4th ed. Great Britain: Pearson Education Publications.

Puddicombe, A. 2011. *Meditation & Mindfulness*. Great Britain: Hodder & Stoughton.

Rock, D. 2008. "SCARF: a Brain-Based Model for Collaborating with and Influencing Others." *NeuroLeadership Journal*, no.1, pp. 1–9.

Schmidt, E., J. Rosenberg, and A. Eagle 2019. *The Trillion Dollar Coach*. New York, NY: Harperbusiness.

Saujani, R. 2019. *Brave, Not Perfect*. United States: Currency.

Sinek, S. 2019. *Start with Why.* Great Britain: Penguin Business.

Soleil, G. 2016. "Workplace Stress: The Health Epidemic of the 21st Century." *huffpost*. https://huffpost.com/entry/workplace-stress-the-heal_b_8923678?guccounter=1&guce_referrer=aHR0cHM6Ly93d3cuZ29vZ2xlLmNvbVS8&guce_referrer_sig=AQAAABX9IIdMatuDM7kD-Cmwku-qh5Wlqyw0jMcNfBF6Iz6vAw2MIOUtCO4m2eZrp-24SBjVhWQ-0_g7zx8_uwKxGa-iOtDet7w5yRHoz4KETIKFYPknpopKcTb9QNc8rDMfetUQNsWTg2hkeeAWdGMMu8cGWxb_3hJ0qTHjNe8OP2go (accessed February 06, 2021).

The American Institute of stress. 2001. "The Quandary of Job Stress Compensation." https://workplacepsychology.files.wordpress.com/2016/07/the-quandary-of-job-stress-compensation_rosch.pdf (accessed February 06, 2021).

Van Den Berg, G., and Pietersma, P. 2009. *Key Management Models*, 2nd ed. United Kingdom: FT Publishing International.

Whitmore, J. 2017. *Coaching for performance*. 5th ed. London: Nicholas Brealey Publishing.

Willink, J., and Babin, L. 2017. *Extreme Ownership*, 2nd ed. Place: New York, NY: St. Martin's Press.

World Health Organization. 2020. "Occupational Health: Stress at the Workplace." https://who.int/news-room/q-a-detail/ccupational-health-stress-at-the-workplace (accessed February 06, 2021).

About the Authors

Simonetta works for an international company as Marketing Director for Global Practices. In her 20-year career she has held various roles in consulting, business development, and marketing in Italy, Europe, and globally. She is an ICF (International Coach Federation)-certified coach and NLP (neuro-linguistic programming) Master Practitioner and has attended courses in neuroscience, science of happiness, and mindfulness in Italy and abroad. In 2020 she founded The Brave Club, a digital community to support women empowerment.

Lucio is the CEO of Crescendo, a business strategy, digital transformation, and go-to-market consulting firm. He is in the board of directors of several companies and is a senior lecturer at some Italian and foreign universities. Previously, he was the VP of strategy and marketing at Hewlett Packard.

Index

www.ingramcontent.com/pod-product-compliance
Lightning Source LLC
Chambersburg PA
CBHW061328220326
41599CB00026B/5086